Easy Cooking With 5 Ingredients

Appetizers & Beverages
Breads, Brunch & Breakfast
Soups, Salads & Sandwiches
Vegetables & Side Dishes
Main Dishes
Sweets

Recipes with 5 ingredients made in 3 easy steps.

By
Barbara C. Jones

Published By
Cookbook Resources
Highland Village, Texas

Easy Cooking with 5 Ingredients

1st Printing   October 2001
2nd Printing   July 2002
3rd Printing   November 2002
4th Printing   January 2003
5th Printing   September 2004
6th Printing   February 2005
7th Printing   October 2005

ISBN 1-931294-86-0 (Hard Bound)
Library of Congress Number 2004115661
ISBN 1-931294-87-9 (Paper Back)
Library of Congress Number 2004115660

Illustrations by Nancy Murphy Griffith.

Edited, Designed and Published in the
United States of America by
Cookbook Resources, LLC
541 Doubletree Drive
Highland Village, Texas 75077
Toll free 866-229-2665
www.cookbookresources.com
Manufactured in China

cookbook resources LLC
Bringing Family And Friends To The Table

INTRODUCTION

We are all in a hurry today and *Easy Cooking with 5 Ingredients* is the "hurry up" way to great meals, easy cooking and the best way to get those compliments from family and friends. Raves are in order when you make the Unbelievable Crab Dip, the Quick Onion-Guacamole Dip or the Fiesta Dip. Crabmeat is the wonderful seafood that is just as good canned or fresh. And the Fiesta Dip has a little different twist to the typical Mexican Dip. The Juicy Fruit Dip is spectacular and nectarines are so good. Try it with apples or bananas and you will be feeding the family lots of delicious fruit. Stretch your world to the luscious mango and papaya – eating healthy at the same time. The Tropical Mango Salad is hard to beat!

Whoever heard of spinach sandwiches? They are delicious, creamy and flavorful – perfect for home or afternoon snack. You'll never go wrong on the Butter-Mint Salad – it has a fabulous Hawaiian flavor and goes well with any entrée. It is so good you could even use it as a dessert.

Now when your looking for a wonderful chicken dinner for family or friends, the Chicken Marseilles will set your meal apart while taking only a few minutes to "put together". And the Green Bean Revenge will call for a large glass of cold water, but the "hot and spicy" will put your tastebuds in high gear. Mash potatoes are usually family fare, but Creamy Mashed Potatoes will give the potatoes a company taste. And when you are looking for the extra special company flair, try the Chicken Olé or the Carnival Couscous. The couscous has your colorful vegetables and makes a really special dish. For the great ending, the Sunny Lime Pie or the Apricot Cobbler are so quick and easy to make (and good), you'll put it on the menu often.

How many times have you needed to rush foods to the home of a friend in need? The Favorite Cake will be the one you choose – and all the ingredients can be kept on your pantry shelf (except the eggs, but you will have them in the refrigerator). Your *Easy Cooking With 5 Ingredients Cookbook* will give you lots of ideas for "easy fixin" foods to take to that best friend, your church or the party where everybody pitches in.

"Dig In" to the cookbook with great dishes that have only 5 ingredients and give you 3 easy steps to "kitchen fame".

Barbara C. Jones

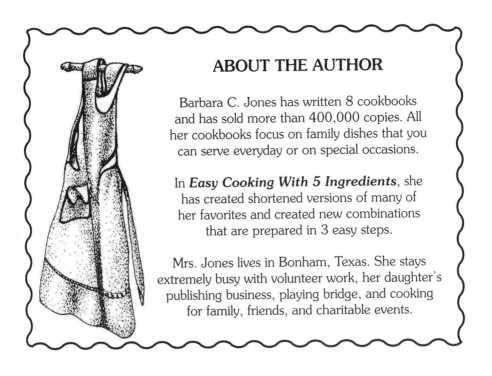

ABOUT THE AUTHOR

Barbara C. Jones has written 8 cookbooks and has sold more than 400,000 copies. All her cookbooks focus on family dishes that you can serve everyday or on special occasions.

In *Easy Cooking With 5 Ingredients*, she has created shortened versions of many of her favorites and created new combinations that are prepared in 3 easy steps.

Mrs. Jones lives in Bonham, Texas. She stays extremely busy with volunteer work, her daughter's publishing business, playing bridge, and cooking for family, friends, and charitable events.

Table of Contents

Notes

APPETIZERS
&
BEVERAGES

Hurrah for Shrimp

1 (8 ounce) package cream cheese, softened	1 (228 g)
½ cup mayonnaise	125 ml
1 (6 ounce) can tiny, cooked shrimp, drained	1 (170 g)
1¼ teaspoons creole (or cajun) seasoning	6 ml
1 tablespoon lemon juice	15 ml

1. Blend cream cheese and mayonnaise in mixing bowl, until creamy.
2. Add shrimp, seasoning and lemon juice; whip only until well mixed.
3. Serve with chips.

The Creole (or Cajun) seasoning is the key to this great dip!

Favorite Stand-By Shrimp Dip

2 cups cooked, veined shrimp, finely chopped	500 ml
2 tablespoons horseradish	30 ml
½ cup chili sauce	125 ml
¾ cup mayonnaise	180 ml
1 tablespoon lemon juice	15 ml

1. Combine all ingredients with a few sprinkles of salt and refrigerate. (If shrimp has been frozen, be sure to drain well.)
2. Serve with cucumber or zucchini slices.

Fiesta Dip

1 (15 ounce) can tamales	1 (438 g)
1 (16 ounce) can chili without beans	1 (454 g)
1 cup picante sauce	250 ml
2 (5 ounce) jars processed cheese spread	2 (142 g)
1 cup finely chopped onion	250 ml

1. Mash tamales with fork.
2. In saucepan, combine all ingredients and heat to mix.
3. Serve hot with crackers or chips.

Unbelievable Crab Dip

1 (16 ounce) package cubed processed cheese	1 (454 g)
2 (6.5 ounce) cans crabmeat, drained, picked	2 (184 g)
1 bunch fresh green onions with tops, chopped	1
2 cups mayonnaise	500 ml
½ teaspoon seasoned salt	2 ml

1. Melt cheese in top of double boiler. Add remaining ingredients.
2. Serve hot (or room temperature) with assorted crackers. Absolutely delicious!

Don't count on your guest leaving the dip table until this dip is gone!

Jump-In Crab Dip

1 (6 ounce) can white crabmeat	1 (170 g)
1 (8 ounce) package cream cheese	1 (228 g)
½ cup (1 stick) butter (the real thing)	125 ml

1. In saucepan, combine crabmeat, cream cheese and butter. Heat and mix thoroughly.
2. Transfer to hot chafing dish. Serve with chips.

This is so good you will wish you had doubled the recipe!

Crab-Dip Kick

1 (8 ounce) package cream cheese, softened	1 (228 g)
3 tablespoons salsa	45 ml
2 tablespoons prepared horseradish	30 ml
1 (6 ounce) can crabmeat, drained, flaked	1 (170 g)

1. In mixing bowl, beat cream cheese until creamy; add salsa and horseradish and mix well.
2. Stir in crabmeat and refrigerate. Serve with assorted crackers.

Hot Broccoli Dip

1 (16 ounce) box Mexican processed cheese	1 (454 g)
1 (10 ounce) can golden mushroom soup	1 (284 g)
1 (10 ounce) box frozen chopped broccoli, thawed	1 (284 g)

1. In saucepan over medium heat, combine cheese and soup. Stir constantly until cheese melts.
2. Stir broccoli into cheese-soup mixture.
3. Serve hot with chips.

Zippy Broccoli-Cheese Dip

1 (10 ounce) package frozen chopped broccoli, thawed, drained	1 (284 g)
2 tablespoons butter	30 ml
2 ribs celery, chopped	2
1 small onion, finely chopped	1
1 (16 ounce) package cubed mild Mexican processed cheese	1 (454 g)

1. Make sure broccoli is thoroughly thawed and drained. Place butter in large saucepan and saute broccoli, celery and onion at medium heat for about 5 minutes, stirring several times.
2. Add cheese and heat, stirring constantly, just until cheese melts.
3. Serve hot with chips.

If you want the "zip" to be zippier, use hot Mexican processed cheese instead of the mild.

Spicy Beef and Cheese Dip

1 (10 ounce) can tomatoes and green chilies	1 (284 g)
½ teaspoon garlic powder	2 ml
2 (16 ounce) packages cubed processed cheese	2 (454 g)
1 pound lean ground beef, browned, cooked	454 g

1. In large saucepan, place tomatoes and green chilies, garlic and cubed. (Use Mexican processed if you like it really spicy.) Heat on low until cheese melts.
2. Add ground beef and mix well.
3. Serve with tortilla chips.

Hot Sombrero Dip

2 (15 ounce) cans bean dip	2 (438 g)
1 pound lean ground beef, browned, cooked	454 g
1 (4 ounce) can green chilies	1 (115 g)
1 cup hot salsa	250 ml
1½ cups shredded cheddar cheese	375 ml

1. Layer bean dip, ground beef, chilies and picante sauce in a 3-quart (3 L) baking dish. Top with cheese.
2. Bake at 350° (176° C) just until cheese melts, about 10 or 15 minutes.
3. Serve with tortilla chips.

Spinach-Cheese Dip

1 (10 ounce) package frozen chopped spinach, thawed	1 (284 g)
2 (8 ounce) packages cream cheese, softened	2 (228 g)
1 (1.2 ounce) package dry vegetable soup mix	1 (30 g)
1 (8 ounce) can water chestnuts, chopped	1 (228 g)

1. Drain spinach on several paper towels. Squeeze or mash spinach into towels several times to make sure all water is gone from spinach.
2. In mixing bowl, beat cream cheese until smooth. Fold in the spinach, soup mix and water chestnuts and chill.
3. Serve with chips or crackers.

I have listed 3 dips that are basically spinach dips. All 3
(Spinach Cheese Dip, Vegetable Dip and Green Wonder Dip)
are a little different – creamy, crunchy or spicy and they are
all great. Even spinach haters will like these dips.

Veggie Dip

1 (10 ounce) package frozen chopped spinach, thawed, WELL drained	1 (284 g)
1 bunch chopped fresh green onions with tops, chopped	1
1 (.9 ounce) envelop dry vegetable soup mix	1 (26 g)
1 tablespoon lemon juice	15 ml
2 (8 ounce) cartons sour cream	2 (228 g)

1. Drain spinach on several paper towels.
2. In medium bowl, combine all ingredients adding a little salt. (Adding several drops of hot sauce is also good.) Cover and refrigerate.
3. Serve with chips.

You will have the family saying "You mean this is spinach!"

Green Wonder Dip

1 (10 ounce) package frozen, chopped spinach, thawed	1 (284 g)
1 (1⅛ ounce) package dry vegetable soup mix	1 (42 g)
½ cup minced onion	125 ml
1 cup mayonnaise	250 ml
1 cup sour cream	250 ml

1. Drain spinach well by pressing out all excess water. (Using paper towels is the best way to get all excess water out of spinach.)
2. Combine all ingredients and mix well. Cover and refrigerate overnight.
3. Serve with crackers, chips or raw vegetable sticks.

The Big Dipper

1 (15 ounce) can chili (no beans)	1 (438 g)
1 (10 ounce) can tomatoes and green chilies	1 (284 g)
1 (16 ounce) package cubed processed cheese	1 (454 g)
½ cup chopped green onions	125 ml
½ teaspoon cayenne pepper	2 ml

1. In saucepan, combine all ingredients. Heat just until cheese melts, stirring constantly.
2. Serve warm with assorted dippers or toasted French bread sticks.

Sassy Onion Dip

1 (8 ounce) package cream cheese, softened	1 (284 g)
1 (8 ounce) carton sour cream	1 (284 g)
½ cup chili sauce	125 ml
1 (1 ounce) package dry onion soup mix	1 (28 g)
1 tablespoon lemon juice	15 ml

1. In mixing bowl, beat cream cheese until fluffy. Add remaining ingredients and mix well.
2. Cover and chill. Serve with strips of raw zucchini, celery, carrots, etc.

Plain and simple, but great!

Pizza-In-A-Bowl

1 pound lean ground beef	454 g
1 (26 ounce) jar marinara or spaghetti sauce	1 (742 g)
2 teaspoons dried oregano	10 ml
1 (16 ounce) package shredded mozzarella cheese	1 (454 g)
¾ teaspoon garlic powder	4 ml

1. In a saucepan, cook beef over medium heat until no longer pink; drain.
2. Stir in marinara sauce and oregano; simmer about 15 minutes. Gradually stir in cheese until it melts.
3. Pour into a fondue pot or small slow cooker to keep warm. Serve with Italian toast (Panetini – found in the deli).

Monterey Jack's Dip

1 (8 ounce) package cream cheese, softened, whipped	1 (228 g)
1 (16 ounce) can chili (no beans)	1 (454 g)
1 (4 ounce) can diced green chilies	1 (115 g)
1 (8 ounce) package grated Monterey Jack cheese	1 (228 g)
1 (4 ounce) can chopped black olives	1 (115 g)

1. In 7 x 11-inch (18 x 28 cm) glass baking dish, layer cream cheese, chili, chilies, cheese and black olives.
2. Bake uncovered at 325° (163° C) for 30 minutes.
3. Serve with chips.

Hot Corn Dip

1 (15 ounce) can whole kernel corn, drained	1 (438 g)
1 (7 ounce) can chopped green chilies, drained	1 (198 g)
½ cup chopped sweet red pepper	125 ml
1½ cups shredded colby and Monterey Jack cheese	375 ml
¼ cup mayonnaise	60 ml

1. In bowl, combine corn, chilies, red pepper and cheeses. Stir in mayonnaise. Adding ½ cup (125 ml) chopped walnuts makes this dip even better.)
2. Transfer to ungreased 2-quart (2 L) baking dish.
3. Cover and bake at 325° (163° C) for 35 minutes. Serve hot with tortilla chips.

Sometimes green chilies are not very hot so I like to add a pinch or two of red pepper.

Quick Mix Dip

1 (8 ounce) package cream cheese, softened	1 (228 g)
1 cup mayonnaise	250 ml
1 (1 ounce) package ranch-style salad dressing mix	1 (28 g)
½ onion, finely minced	½

1. In mixing bowl, combine cream cheese and mayonnaise and beat until creamy.
2. Stir in salad dressing mix and onion.
3. Chill and serve with fresh vegetables.

Ham It Up

2 (8 ounce) packages cream cheese, softened	**2 (228 g)**
2 (2.5 ounce) cans deviled ham	**2 (70 g)**
2 heaping tablespoons horseradish	**30 ml**
¼ cup minced onion	**60 ml**
¼ cup finely chopped celery	**60 ml**

1. In mixing bowl, beat cream cheese until creamy.
2. Add all other ingredients
3. Chill and serve with crackers. (This would also make little party sandwiches with party rye bread.)

Ham-It-Up-Some-More Dip

1 (16 ounce) carton small curd cottage cheese	**1 (454 g)**
2 (6 ounce) cans deviled ham	**2 (170 g)**
1 (1 ounce) package dry onion soup mix	**1 (28 g)**
½ cup sour cream	**125 ml**
2 tablespoons lemon juice	**30 ml**

1. Blend cottage cheese in blender or mixer.
2. Add ham, soup mix, sour cream and lemon juice and mix well.
3. Serve with crackers.

I like to add a little "zip" in this dip by adding several dashes of hot sauce.

Creamy Dilly Dip

1 (8 ounce) carton sour cream	1 (228 g)
1 cup mayonnaise,	250 ml
2 tablespoons lemon juice	30 ml
4 green onions with tops, chopped	4
1 tablespoon dill weed	15 ml
2 teaspoons white wine worcestershire sauce	10 ml

1. Combine all ingredients until well blended. (Do not use the darker worcestershire. White wine worcestershire keeps this dip light in color and texture.)
2. Sprinkle lightly with paprika for color. Cover and refrigerate.
3. Serve with carrot sticks, broccoli flowerets or jicama sticks.

Curry Lover's Veggie Dip

1 cup mayonnaise	250 ml
½ cup sour cream	125 ml
1 teaspoon curry powder	10 ml
¼ teaspoon hot sauce	1 ml
1 teaspoon lemon juice	5 ml

1. Combine all ingredients and mix until well blended.
2. Sprinkle a little paprika for color. Cover and refrigerate. Serve with raw vegetables.

Roquefort Dip

1 (8 ounce) package cream cheese, softened	1 (228 g)
2 cups mayonnaise	500 ml
1 small onion, finely grated	1
1 (3 ounce) package roquefort cheese, crumbled	1 (85 g)
⅛ teaspoon garlic powder	.5 ml

1. In mixing bowl, combine cream cheese and mayonnaise. Beat until creamy.
2. Add onion, roquefort cheese and garlic powder and mix well. Refrigerate.
3. Serve with zucchini sticks, turnip sticks or cauliflower flowerets.

Veggie Dive Dip

1 cup mayonnaise	250 ml
1 (8 ounce) carton sour cream	1 (228 g)
1½ teaspoons seasoned salt	7 ml
1 teaspoon dill weed,	5 ml
2 tablespoons parsley	30 ml
1 bunch green onions with tops, chopped	1

1. Stir all ingredients together and chill. Better if made a day ahead.
2. Serve with celery sticks, broccoli flowerets, jicama sticks or carrot sticks.

La Cucaracha

1 (12 ounce) package chorizo, sliced or cut up	1 (340 g)
1 (16 ounce) package Mexican-style processed cheese	1 (454 g)
1 (15 ounce) can stewed tomatoes	1 (438 g)

1. Saute chorizo, cook and drain.
2. In double boiler, on medium heat, melt cheese and tomatoes, stirring constantly.
3. Combine chorizo, cheese and tomatoes and mix well. Serve with tortilla chips.

California Clam Dip

1 (1 ounce) envelope dry onion soup mix	1 (28 g)
2 (8 ounce) cartons sour cream	2 (228 g)
1 (7 ounce) can minced clams, drained	1 (198 g)
3 tablespoons chili sauce	45 ml
1 tablespoon lemon juice	15 ml

1. Combine onion soup mix and sour cream and mix well.
2. Add clams, chili sauce and lemon juice.
3. Chill. Serve with assorted crackers.

Zesty Clam Dip

1 (15 ounce) can New England clam chowder	1 (438 g)
1 (8 ounce) and 1 (3 ounce) package	1 (228 g)
cream cheese, softened	1 (85 g)
2 tablespoons minced onion	30 ml
2 tablespoons prepared horseradish	30 ml
2 tablespoons white wine worcestershire	30 ml

1. Combine all ingredients and blend in food processor until smooth.
2. Serve with raw vegetables or chips.

———————★———————

Roasted Garlic Dip

4 or 5 unpeeled whole garlic cloves	4 or 5
2 (8 ounce) packages cream cheese, softened	2 (228 g)
¾ cup mayonnaise	180 ml
1 (7 or 9 ounce) jar sweet roasted red	
peppers, drained, coarsely chopped	1 (228 g)
1 bunch fresh green onions with tops,	
chopped	1

1. Preheat oven to 400° (204° C). Lightly brush outside of garlic bulbs with a little oil and place in shallow baking pan. Heat about 10 minutes. Cool. Press roasted garlic out of cloves.
2. Beat cream cheese and mayonnaise until creamy. Add remaining ingredients and mix well. (Roasted peppers are great in this recipe, but if you want it a little spicy, add several drops of hot sauce.)
3. Sprinkle with red pepper or paprika and serve with chips.

Great Guacamole

4 avocados, peeled	4
About ½ cup salsa	125 ml
¼ cup sour cream	60 ml
1 teaspoon salt	5 ml

1. Split avocados and remove seeds. Mash avocado with fork.
2. Add salsa, sour cream and salt.
3. Serve with tortilla chips.

Place one of the avocado seeds in the dip until time
to serve – the seed keeps the color bright.

Avocado and Onion Dip

1 (1 ounce) package golden onion soup mix	1 (28 g)
1 (8 ounce) carton sour cream	1 (228 g)
½ cup mayonnaise	125 ml
2 ripe avocados, mashed	2
1 tablespoon lemon juice	15 ml

1. Mix all ingredients and work quickly so avocados won't turn dark.
2. Serve with wheat crackers.

Quick Onion Guacamole

1 (8 ounce) carton sour cream	1 (228 g)
1 (1 ounce) package dry onion soup mix	1 (28 g)
2 (8 ounce) cartons avocado dip	2 (228 g)
2 green onions with tops, chopped	2
½ teaspoon crushed dill weed	2 ml

1. Mix all ingredients and chill.
2. Serve with chips.

Tasty Tuna

1 (6 ounce) can solid white tuna, drained, flaked	1 (170 g)
1 (1 ounce) envelope dry zesty Italian salad dressing mix	1 (28 g)
1 tablespoon lemon juice	15 ml
1 (8 ounce) carton sour cream	1 (228 g)
3 green onions with tops, chopped	3

1. Combine all ingredients and stir until blended. Chill.
2. Serve with melba rounds.

Cucumber Dip

2 medium cucumbers	**2**
2 (8 ounce) packages cream cheese, softened	**2 (228 g)**
Several drops hot sauce	
1 (1 ounce) package ranch salad dressing mix	**1 (28 g)**
½ teaspoon garlic powder	**2 ml**

1. Peel cucumbers, cut in half lengthwise and scoop out seeds. Chop cucumbers in very fine pieces (or in a food processor). In mixer, combine cream cheese, hot sauce, dressing mix and garlic powder and beat until creamy.
2. Combine cucumbers and cream cheese mixture and mix well. (Add ½ cup (125 ml) chopped pecans to make this dip even better.) Serve with chips.

This dip makes great "party" sandwiches made with thin sliced white bread. If you do use it for sandwiches, make sure you squeeze all the water out of the cucumbers.

Poor Man's Pate

1 (16 ounce) roll braunschweiger, room temperature	**1 (454 g)**
1 (1 ounce) package onion soup mix	**1 (28 g)**
1 (8 ounce) carton sour cream	**1 (228 g)**
1 (8 ounce) package cream cheese, softened	**1 (228 g)**
Several dashes hot sauce	

1. Mash braunschweiger (goose liver) with fork.
2. With mixer, beat remaining ingredients until fairly creamy.
3. Add braunschweiger and mix well. Refrigerate. Serve with chips.

Sweet Onions

5 Texas 1015 or Vidalia sweet onions, chopped	**5**
1 cup sugar	**250 ml**
½ cup white vinegar	**125 ml**
⅔ cup mayonnaise	**160 ml**
1 teaspoon celery salt	**5 ml**

1. Soak onions in sugar, vinegar and 2 cups (500 ml) water for about 3 hours. Drain.
2. Toss with mayonnaise and celery salt.
3. Serve on crackers.

Cheese Strips

1 loaf thin-sliced bread	**1**
1 (8 ounce) package shredded cheddar cheese	**1 (228 g)**
6 slices bacon, fried, drained, coarsely broken	**6**
½ cup chopped onion	**125 ml**
1 cup mayonnaise	**250 ml**

1. Remove crust from bread. Combine next 4 ingredients and spread filling over slices; cut into 3 strips. Place on cookie sheet.
2. Bake at 400° (204° C) for 10 minutes.
3. For a special touch, add ⅓ cup (80 ml) slivered almonds, toasted.

Blue Cheese Crisps

2 (4 ounce) packages crumbled blue cheese	2 (115 g)
½ cup (1 stick) butter, softened	125 ml
1⅓ cups flour	330 ml
⅓ cup poppy seeds	80 ml
¼ teaspoon ground red pepper	1 ml

1. Beat blue cheese and butter at medium speed until fluffy. Add flour, poppy seeds and red pepper and beat until blended.
2. Divide dough in half; shape each portion into 9-inch (23 cm) log. Cover and refrigerate 2 hours.
3. Cut each log into ¼-inch (.5 cm) slices and place on ungreased baking sheet. Bake at 350° (176° C) for 13 to 15 minutes or until golden brown. Cool.

Party Smokies

1 cup ketchup	250 ml
1 cup plum jelly	250 ml
1 tablespoon lemon juice	15 ml
4 tablespoons prepared mustard	60 ml
2 (5 ounce) packages tiny smoked sausages	2 (142 g)

1. In saucepan, combine all ingredients except sausages, heat and mix well.
2. Add sausages and simmer for 10 minutes.
3. Serve hot with cocktail toothpicks.

Sausage-Pineapple Bits

1 pound link sausage, cooked, skinned	454 g
1 pound hot bulk sausage	454 g
1 (15 ounce) can crushed pineapple with juice	1 (438 g)
2 cups packed brown sugar	500 ml
1 tablespoon white wine worcestershire	15 ml

1. Slice link sausage into ⅓-inch (.5 cm) pieces. Shape bulk sausage into 1-inch (2.5 cm) balls. In skillet, brown sausage balls.
2. In large saucepan, combine pineapple, brown sugar and white wine worcestershire
3. Heat and add both sausages. Simmer for 30 minutes. Serve in chafing dish or small crock pot with cocktail picks.

The "sweet and hot" combination makes a delicious treat.

Sausage Balls

2 cups biscuit mix	500 ml
1 pound hot sausage	454 g
1 cup shredded cheddar cheese	250 ml

1. Combine biscuit mix, sausage and cheese with wooden spoon or with your hands.
2. Shape into 1-inch (2.5 cm) balls, place on cookie sheet and bake at 350° (176° C) for about 20 minutes. These will freeze nicely.

Raspberry-Glazed Wings

¾ cup seedless raspberry jam	180 ml
¼ cup cider vinegar	60 ml
¼ cup soy sauce	60 ml
1 teaspoon garlic powder	5 ml
16 whole chicken wings (about 3 pounds)	16

1. In saucepan, combine jam, vinegar, soy sauce, garlic and 1 teaspoon (5 ml) black pepper. Bring to a boil; boil 1 minute.
2. Cut chicken wings into 3 sections and discard wing tips. Place wings in large bowl, add raspberry mixture and toss to coat. Cover and refrigerate for 4 hours.
3. Line 10 x 15-inch (25 x 38 cm) baking pan with foil and grease foil. Use a slotted spoon to place wings in pan and reserve marinade.
4. Bake uncovered at 350° (176° C) for 30 minutes, turning once. Cook reserved marinade for 10 minutes, brush over wings and bake 25 minutes longer.

Curried Wings

10 chicken wings	10
¼ cup (½ stick) butter, melted	60 ml
¼ cup honey	60 ml
¼ cup prepared mustard	60 ml
1¼ teaspoons curry powder	6 ml

1. Cut off wing tips and discard. Cut wings in half at joint.
2. Combine next 4 ingredients in large zip-top plastic bag. Add chicken and seal. Refrigerate at least 2 hours, turning chicken occasionally.
3. Remove chicken from marinade and discard marinade. Place chicken in greased 9 x 13-inch (23 x 33 cm) baking dish. Bake uncovered at 325° (163° C) for 1 hour.

Cocktail Ham Roll-Ups

1 (3 ounce) package cream cheese, softened	**1 (85 g)**
1 teaspoon finely grated onion	**5 ml**
Mayonnaise	
1 (3 ounce) package sliced ham	**1 (85 g)**
1 (15 ounce) can asparagus spears	**1 (438 g)**

1. Combine cream cheese, grated onion and enough mayonnaise to make spreading consistency.
2. Separate sliced ham, spread mixture on slices and place an asparagus spear (or two) on ham and roll. Cut each roll into 4 pieces.
3. Spear each piece with toothpick for serving. Refrigerate.

This can also be used when serving a salad luncheon – perhaps serving these Ham Roll-Ups (not cutting into pieces), the Broccoli-Cauliflower Salad and the Tropical Mango Salad.

Cheese Straws

1 (5 ounce) package piecrust mix	**1 (142 g)**
¾ cup finely shredded cheddar cheese	**180 ml**
Cayenne pepper	

1. Prepare piecrust according to package directions. Roll out into rectangular shape. Sprinkle cheese over dough. Press cheese into dough. Sprinkle cayenne pepper over cheese. Fold dough over once to cover cheese.
2. Roll out to make ¼-inch (.5 cm) thickness. Cut dough into half by 3-inch (7.5 cm) strips and place on lightly greased cookie sheet.
3. Bake at 350° (176° C) for 12 to 15 minutes or until light brown.

Green Eyes

4 medium dill pickles	**4**
4 slices boiled ham	**4**
Light cream cheese, softened	
Black pepper	

1. Dry off pickles. Lightly coat one side of ham slices with cream cheese and sprinkle on a little pepper. Roll the pickle up in ham slice coated with cream cheese.
2. Chill. Slice into circles to serve.

Here's lookin' at ya!

Kids' Dogs

1 (10 count) package of wieners	**10**
3 cans biscuits (with 10 biscuits per can)	**3**
Dijon mustard	

1. Cut each wiener in thirds. Flatten each biscuit slightly and spread with mustard.
2. Wrap each wiener piece in biscuit and pinch to seal.
3. Bake at 400° (204° C) for 10 to 12 minutes or until light brown.

A kid's favorite!

Chestnuts Under Wraps

1 (8 ounce) can whole water chestnuts, drained	**1 (228 g)**
¼ cup soy sauce	**60 ml**
About ½ pound bacon, cut in thirds	**228 g**

1. Marinate water chestnuts for 1 hour in soy sauce. Wrap ⅓ slice bacon around water chestnut and fasten with tooth pick.
2. Bake at 375° (190° C) for 20 minutes or until bacon is done. Drain and serve hot.

Mini-Reubens

½ cup thousand island dressing	**125 ml**
24 slices party rye bread	**24**
1⅓ cups well-drained chopped sauerkraut	**330 ml**
½ pound thinly sliced corned beef	**228 g**
¼ pound sliced Swiss cheese	**115 g**

1. Spread dressing on slices of bread. Place 1 slice corned beef on bread and top with sauerkraut.
2. Cut cheese the size of bread and place over sauerkraut.
3. Place open-face sandwiches on cookie sheet. Bake at 375° (190° C) for 10 minutes or until cheese melts.

Chicken Lickers

2 white onions, sliced	2
10 to 12 chicken livers	10 to 12
4 strips bacon	4
⅓ cup sherry	80 ml

1. Place onion slices in shallow pan. Top each onion slice with chicken liver and ⅓ strip bacon. Pour sherry over all.
2. Bake uncovered at 350° (176° C) for about 45 minutes or until bacon is crisp. Baste occasionally with pan drippings.

Oyster-Bacon Bites

1 (5 ounce) can smoked oysters, drained, chopped	1 (142 g)
⅔ cup herb-seasoned stuffing mix, crushed	160 ml
¼ cup water	60 ml
8 slices bacon, halved, partially cooked	8

1. Combine oysters, stuffing mix and water. Add another teaspoon water if mixture seems too dry. Form into balls, using about 1 tablespoon (15 ml) mixture for each.
2. Wrap half slice of bacon around each and secure with toothpick. Place on rack in shallow baking pan.
3. Cook at 350° (176° C) for 25 to 30 minutes or until bacon is crisp.

Drunk Franks

1 (10 count) package wieners	**10**
½ cup chili sauce	**125 ml**
½ cup packed brown sugar	**125 ml**
½ cup bourbon	**125 ml**

1. Cut wieners into bite-size pieces. Combine chili sauce, sugar and bourbon in saucepan. Add wieners to sauce and simmer 30 minutes.
2. Serve in chafing dish.

Cheddar Puffs

½ cup (1 stick) butter, softened	**125 ml**
1 cup grated cheddar cheese	**250 ml**
1¼ cups flour	**310 ml**
¼ teaspoon salt	**60 ml**

1. Blend butter and cheese until fairly smooth. Stir in flour and salt. Knead lightly with hands. Roll, 1 teaspoon (5 ml) at a time, into balls.
2. Place on cookie sheet.
3. Bake at 375° (190° C) for 14 to 15 minutes or until golden. Serve hot.

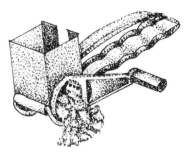

No-Fuss Meatballs

1 (14 ounce) package frozen cooked meatballs, thawed	1 (420 g)
1 tablespoon soy sauce	15 ml
½ cup chili sauce	125 ml
⅔ cup grape jelly or plum jelly	160 ml
¼ cup dijon mustard	60 ml

1. In skillet, cook meatballs in soy sauce until heated.
2. Combine chili sauce, jelly and mustard and pour over meatballs. Cook and stir until jelly dissolves and mixture comes to a boil.
3. Reduce heat, cover and simmer for about 5 minutes.

Sausage Rounds

1 (8 ounce) package crescent dinner rolls	1 (228 g)
1 pound sausage, uncooked	454 g

1. Open package of rolls, smooth out dough with rolling pin and seal the seams.
2. Break up sausage with hands and spread thin layer of sausage over rolls. Roll into log. Wrap in wax paper and freeze several hours.
3. Slice into ¼-inch (.5 cm) rounds. Place on cookie sheet and bake at 350° (176° C) for 20 minutes or until light brown.

The Queen's Cheese Balls

½ cup (1 stick) butter, softened	125 ml
1 (6 ounce) jar sharp processed cheese spread, softened	1 (170 g)
¼ teaspoon cayenne pepper	1 ml
½ teaspoon salt	2 ml
1 cup plus 2 tablespoons flour	250 ml + 30 ml

1. In bowl, mix all ingredients and work in flour gradually.
2. Form into marble-size balls and flatten with fork.
3. Bake at 400° (204° C) for 6 to 8 minutes or until light brown.

Olive-Cheese Balls

2¼ cups shredded sharp cheddar cheese	560 ml
1 cup flour	250 ml
½ cup (1 stick) butter, melted	125 ml
1 (5 ounce) jar green olives	1 (142 g)

1. In large bowl, combine cheese and flour. Add butter and mix well.
2. Cover olives with mixture and form balls.
3. Bake at 350° (176° C) for about 15 minutes or until light brown.

Artichoke-Caviar Delights

2 (8 ounce) packages cream cheese, softened	2 (228 g)
1 (14 ounce) can artichoke hearts, drained, chopped	1 (420 g)
½ cup finely grated onion	125 ml
1 (3 ounce) jar caviar, drained	1 (85 g)
3 hard-boiled eggs, grated	3

1. Beat cream cheese until smooth and add artichoke hearts and onion.
2. Spread in 8 or 9-inch (23 cm) glass pie plate and chill.
3. Before serving, spread caviar on top of cream cheese mixture and place grated egg on top. Serve with crackers.

Hot Artichoke Spread

1 (14 ounce) can artichoke hearts, drained, finely chopped	1 (420 g)
1 (4 ounce) can chopped green chilies	1 (115 g)
1 cup mayonnaise	250 ml
1 (8 ounce) package shredded mozzarella cheese	1 (228 g)
½ teaspoon garlic powder	2 ml

1. Remove any spikes or tough leaves from artichoke hearts.
2. Combine all ingredients and mix thoroughly. Pour into 9-inch (23 cm) square baking pan and sprinkle some paprika over top.
3. Bake at 325° (163° C) for 25 minutes. Serve hot with assorted crackers.

Black Olive Spread

1 (8 ounce) package cream cheese, softened	1 (228 g)
½ cup mayonnaise	125 ml
1 (4 ounce) can chopped black olives	1 (115 g)
3 green onions, chopped very fine	3

1. Whip cream cheese and mayonnaise until smooth. Add olives and onions and chill.
2. Spread on slices of party rye.

Jiffy Tuna Spread

1 (7 ounce) can white tuna, drained, flaked	1 (198 g)
½ cup chopped ripe olives	125 ml
1 (1 ounce) package dry Italian salad dressing mix	1 (28 g)
1 (8 ounce) carton sour cream	1 (228 g)

1. Combine all ingredients and mix well.
2. Sprinkle with a little paprika for color and serve on crackers.

Walnut-Cheese Spread

¾ cup walnuts, chopped	180 ml
1 (16 ounce) package shredded cheddar cheese	1 (454 g)
3 green onions with tops, chopped	3
½ to ¾ cup mayonnaise	125 to 180 ml
½ teaspoon liquid smoke	2 ml

1. Roast walnuts at 250° (121° C) for 10 minutes.
2. Combine all ingredients and let stand in refrigerator overnight.
3. Spread on assorted crackers.

Smoked-Oyster Spread

1 (8 ounce) package cream cheese, softened	1 (228 g)
3 tablespoons mayonnaise	45 ml
1 (3½ ounce) can smoked oysters, chopped	1 (100 g)
½ teaspoon onion salt	2 ml
2 tablespoons parmesan cheese	30 ml

1. Whip cream cheese and mayonnaise until creamy.
2. Add oysters, onion salt and cheese.
3. Mix well and dip or spread on crackers.

Spicy Cheese Round

1 pound hot sausage	454 g
1 cup chunky hot salsa	250 g
1 (16 ounce) package cubed processed cheese	1 (454 g)
1 (16 ounce) package shredded sharp cheddar cheese	1 (454 g)
1 (16 ounce) package shredded mild cheddar cheese	1 (454 g)

1. Brown sausage in large roasting pan. Add salsa and ½ teaspoon (2 ml) garlic powder if you like.
2. Add processed cheese and turn burner on low. Stir constantly while cheese melts. Add cheddar cheeses while stirring. (It will be hard to stir, but you must keep stirring to keep cheese from burning.)
3. Pour into bundt pan coated with non-stick vegetable spray. Refrigerate overnight. Unmold onto platter. (It would be nice to place parsley around ring.) To serve, cut slices of cheese mold and serve with wheat crackers.

Ginger-Fruit Dip

1 (3 ounce) package cream cheese, softened	1 (85 g)
1 (7 ounce) jar marshmallow cream	1 (198 g)
½ cup mayonnaise	125 ml
1 teaspoon ground ginger	5 ml
1 teaspoon grated orange rind	5 ml

1. Beat cream cheese at medium speed until smooth, add marshmallow cream and next 3 ingredients, stirring until smooth.
2. Serve with fresh fruit sticks.

Kahlua Fruit Dip

1 (8 ounce) package cream cheese, softened	**1 (228 g)**
1 (8 ounce) carton whipped topping	**1 (228 g)**
⅔ cup packed brown sugar	**160 ml**
⅓ cup kahlua	**80 ml**
1 (8 ounce) carton sour cream	**1 (228 g)**

1. With mixer, whip cream cheese until creamy and fold in whipped topping.
2. Add sugar, kahlua and sour cream and mix well.
3. Refrigerate 24 hours before serving with fresh fruit.

Juicy Fruit Dip

1 (8 ounce) package cream cheese, softened	**1 (228 g)**
2 (7 ounce) cartons marshmallow cream	**2 (198 g)**
½ teaspoon cinnamon	**2 ml**
⅛ teaspoon ground ginger	**.5 ml**

1. With mixer, combine and beat all ingredients. Mix well and refrigerate.
2. Serve with unpeeled slices of nectarines or apple slices. Delicious!

Fruit'n Crackers

1 (8 ounce) package cream cheese, softened	1 (228 g)
2 tablespoons orange juice	30 ml
1½ teaspoons triple sec	7 ml
1 (11 ounce) package wheat crackers	1 (312 g)
Several kiwi fruit	

1. Beat cream cheese, orange juice and triple sec. Lightly toast crackers at 350° (176° C) for 10 minutes. Spread crackers with cream cheese mixture.
2. Decorate tops of crackers with fruit.

Ginger Cream

1 (8 ounce) package cream cheese, softened	1 (228 g)
½ cup (1 stick) unsalted butter, softened	125 ml
2 tablespoons milk	30 ml
3 tablespoons finely chopped crystallized ginger	45 ml

1. Combine all ingredients in mixing bowl. Beat until creamy.
2. Spread on your favorite fruit or nut breads.

Peanut Butter Spread

1 (8 ounce) package cream cheese, softened	1 (228 g)
1⅔ cups creamy peanut butter	410 ml
½ cup powdered sugar	125 ml
1 tablespoon milk	15 ml

1. In mixing bowl, cream all ingredients.
2. Serve spread with apple wedges or graham crackers.

Ambrosia Spread

1 (11 ounce) can mandarin orange sections,
  drained   **1 (312 g)**
1 (8 ounce) container soft cream cheese with
  pineapple, softened   **1 (228 g)**
¼ cup flaked coconut, toasted   **60 ml**
¼ cup slivered almonds, chopped, toasted   **60 ml**

1. Chop orange sections and set aside.
2. Whip cream cheese and fold in coconut and almonds.
3. Spread on date nut bread, banana bread, etc.
   Toast coconut and almonds at 275°
   (135° C) for 10 minutes.

Orange-Cheese Spread

2 (8 ounce) packages cream cheese, softened   **2 (228 g)**
⅔ cup powdered sugar   **160 ml**
1 tablespoon grated orange peel   **15 ml**
2 tablespoons Grand Marnier   **30 ml**
2 tablespoons frozen orange juice concentrate,
  undiluted   **30 ml**

1. Blend all ingredients in mixing bowl until smooth and
   refrigerate.
2. Spread on dessert breads to make sandwiches or use as dip
   for fruit.

Green Olive Spread

1 (8 ounce) package cream cheese, softened	1 (228 g)
⅔ cup mayonnaise	160 ml
¾ cup chopped pecans	180 ml
1 cup green olives, drained, chopped	250 ml
¼ teaspoon black pepper	1 ml

1. In mixing bowl, blend cream cheese and mayonnaise until smooth.
2. Add remaining ingredients, mix well and refrigerate.
3. Serve on crackers or make sandwiches with party rye bread.

Beef or Ham Spread

1 pound leftover roast beef or ham	454 g
¾ cup sweet pickle relish	180 ml
½ onion, finely diced	½
2 celery ribs, chopped	2
2 hard-boiled eggs, chopped	2
Mayonnaise	

1. Chop meat in food processor and add relish, onion, celery and eggs.
2. Add a little salt and pepper. Fold in enough mayonnaise to make mixture spreadable and chill.
3. Spread on crackers or bread for sandwiches.

Chipped Beef Ball

1 (8 ounce) package cream cheese, softened	1 (228 g)
2 teaspoons horseradish	10 ml
1 teaspoon prepared mustard	5 ml
¼ teaspoon garlic powder	1 ml
1 (2.5 ounce) jar dried beef, finely cut up	1 (70 g)

1. In mixing bowl, blend cream cheese, horseradish, mustard and garlic powder. Roll into ball.
2. Roll ball in cut-up dried beef. (The best way to cut up dried beef is with scissors.) Serve with crackers.

Mexican-Cheese Dip

1 (16 ounce) package shredded cheddar cheese	1 (454 g)
1 (5 ounce) can evaporated milk	1 (142 g)
1 teaspoon cumin	5 ml
1 tablespoon chili powder	15 ml
1 (10 ounce) can tomatoes and green chilies	1 (284 g)

1. Melt cheese with evaporated milk in double boiler.
2. In blender, mix cumin, chili powder and tomatoes and green chilies; add a dash of garlic powder if you like.
3. Add tomato mixture to melted cheese and mix well. Serve hot with chips.

Mexican Pick-Up Sticks

1 (7 ounce) can potato sticks	**1 (198 g)**
2 (12 ounce) cans spanish peanuts	**2 (340 g)**
2 (3 ounce) cans french-fried onions	**2 (85 g)**
⅓ cup (5 tablespoons) butter, melted	**80 ml**
1 (1.25 ounce) package taco seasoning dry mix	**1 (70 g)**

1. In 9 x 13-inch (23 x 33 cm) baking dish, combine potato sticks, peanuts and fried onions.
2. Drizzle with melted butter and stir. Sprinkle with taco seasoning and mix well.
3. Bake at 250° (121° C) for 45 minutes, stirring every 15 minutes.

Onion-Guacamole Dip

1 (8 ounce) carton sour cream	**1 (228 g)**
1 (1 ounce) package dry onion soup mix	**1 (28 g)**
2 (8 ounce) cartons avocado dip	**2 (228 g)**
2 green onions with tops, chopped	**2**
½ teaspoon crushed dill weed	**2 ml**

1. Mix all ingredients and chill.
2. Serve with chips.

Tex-Mex Nachos

About 35 tortilla chips	35
1 (8 ounce) package shredded Monterey Jack cheese	1 (228 g)
2 tablespoons sliced jalapeno peppers	30 ml
⅛ teaspoon chili powder	.5 ml
Bean Dip (recipe below)	

1. Arrange chips on 9 x 13-inch (23 x 33 cm) baking dish. Sprinkle with cheese. Top with jalapeno peppers and sprinkle with chili powder.
2. Broil 4 inches from heat until cheese melts.

Bean Dip

1 (15 ounce) can Mexican-style chili beans	1 (438 g)
½ teaspoon ground cumin	2 ml
½ teaspoon chili powder	2 ml
¼ teaspoon dried oregano	1 ml

1. Drain beans and reserve 2 tablespoons (30 ml) liquid. Combine beans, reserved liquid and remaining ingredients in food processor. Pulse several times until beans are partially chopped.
2. Pour mixture into small saucepan and cook over low heat, stirring constantly until thoroughly heated. Serve with Tex-Mex Nachos above.

Tuna-Avocado Dip

2 medium avocados	2
1 (6 ounce) can white tuna, drained	1 (170 g)
½ cup creamed cottage cheese	125 g
2 tablespoons lemon juice	30 ml
Salt and pepper	

1. Peel and cut avocados in chunks.
2. In mixing bowl, combine remaining ingredients and beat. Mixture will not be smooth; a little texture should remain.

Deluxe Pimento Cheese Spread

1 (16 ounce) package shredded sharp cheddar cheese	1 (454 g)
2 (4 ounce) jars diced pimentos, drained	2 (115 g)
1 cup salsa	250 ml
¼ teaspoon freshly ground black pepper	1 ml
3 tablespoons mayonnaise	45 ml

1. In large bowl, combine cheese, pimentos and salsa and mix well.
2. Add pepper and mayonnaise and blend well.
3. Refrigerate. Spread on wheat crackers or use to make sandwiches.

Best Coffee Punch

1 gallon very strong coffee	**4 L**
½ cup sugar	**125 ml**
3 tablespoons vanilla	**45 ml**
2 pints half-and-half cream	**1 L**
1 gallon vanilla ice cream, softened	**4 L**

1. Add sugar to coffee (add more sugar if you like it sweeter) and chill.
2. Add vanilla and half-and-half.
3. When ready to serve, combine coffee mixture and ice cream in punch bowl. Break up ice cream into chunks.

*This is so good you will want a big glass of it
instead of a punch cup full.*

Pineapple-Citrus Punch

1 (46 ounce) can pineapple juice, chilled	**1 (2 kg)**
1 quart apple juice, chilled	**1 L**
1 (2 liter) bottle lemon-lime carbonated beverage, chilled	**1 (2 L)**
1 (6 ounce) can frozen lemonade concentrate, thawed	**1 (170 g)**
1 orange, sliced	**1**

1. Combine first 4 ingredients in punch bowl.
2. Add orange slices for decoration.

Party Punch

1 (46 ounce) can pineapple juice	1 (2 kg)
1 (46 ounce) can apple juice	1 (2 kg)
3 quarts ginger ale, chilled	3 L

1. Freeze pineapple and apple juice in their cans.
2. One hour before serving, set out cans at room temperature.
3. When ready to serve, place pineapple and apple juice in punch bowl and add chilled ginger ale. Stir to mix.

Strawberry Punch

2 (10 ounce) boxes frozen strawberries, thawed	2 (284 g)
2 (6 ounce) cans frozen pink lemonade concentrate	2 (170 g)
2 (2 liter) bottles ginger ale, chilled	2 (2 L)

1. Process strawberries through blender. Pour lemonade into punch bowl and stir in strawberries.
2. Add chilled ginger ale and stir well. It would be nice to make an ice ring out of another bottle of ginger ale.

Creamy Strawberry Punch

1 (10 ounce) package frozen strawberries, thawed	1 (284 g)
½ gallon strawberry ice cream, softened	2 L
2 (2 liter) bottles ginger ale, chilled	2 (2 L)

1. Process strawberries through blender.
2. Combine strawberries, chunks of ice cream and ginger ale in punch bowl. Stir and serve immediately.

Sparkling Cranberry Punch

Ice mold for punch bowl
Red food coloring
2 quarts cranberry juice cocktail, chilled   2 L
1 (6 ounce) can frozen lemonade concentrate,
   thawed   1 (170 g)
1 quart ginger ale, chilled   1 L

1. Pour water in mold for ice ring and add red food coloring to make mold brighter and prettier.
2. Mix cranberry juice and lemonade in pitcher. Refrigerate until ready to serve.
3. When serving, pour cranberry mixture into punch bowl, add ginger ale and stir well. Add ice mold to punch bowl.

Citrus Grove Punch

3 cups sugar   750 ml
6 cups orange juice, chilled   1.5 L
6 cups grapefruit juice, chilled 1.5 L
1½ cups lime juice, chilled   375 ml
1 liter ginger ale, chilled   1 L

1. In saucepan, bring sugar and 2 cups (500 ml) water to boil and cook for 5 minutes. Cover and refrigerate until cool.
2. Combine juices and sugar mixture and mix well.
3. Just before serving, stir in ginger ale. Serve over ice.

Cranberry-Pineapple Punch

1 (48 ounce) bottle cranberry juice drink	1 (2 kg)
1 (48 ounce) can pineapple juice	1 (2 kg)
½ cup sugar	125 ml
2 teaspoons almond extract	10 ml
1 (2 liter) bottle ginger ale, chilled	1 (2 L)

1. Stir cranberry juice, pineapple juice, sugar and almond extract until sugar dissolves. Cover and chill 8 hours.
2. When ready to serve, stir in ginger ale.

Easiest Grape Punch

½ gallon ginger ale	2 L
Red seedless grapes	
Sparkling white grape juice, chilled	

1. Make ice ring of ginger ale and seedless grapes.
2. When ready to serve, pour sparkling white grape juice in punch bowl with ice ring.

Sparkling white grape juice is great just by itself!

Ginger Ale Nectar Punch

1 (12 ounce) cans apricot nectar	1 (340 g)
1 (6 ounce) can frozen orange juice	
concentrate, thawed, undiluted	1 (170 g)
1 cup water	250 ml
2 tablespoons lemon juice	30 ml
1 (2 liter) bottle ginger ale, chilled	1 (2 L)

1. Combine first 4 ingredients and chill.
2. When ready to serve, stir in ginger ale.

Mocha Punch

4 cups brewed coffee	1 L
¼ cup sugar	60 ml
4 cups milk	1 L
4 cups chocolate ice cream, softened	1 L

1. Combine coffee and sugar and stir until sugar dissolves.
   Refrigerate for 2 hours.
2. Just before serving, pour into punch bowl. Add milk and mix
   well. Top with scoops of ice cream and stir well.

Instant Cocoa Mix

1 (8 quart) box dry milk powder	1 (8 L
1 (12 ounce) jar non-dairy creamer	1 (340 g)
1 (16 ounce) can instant chocolate-flavored	
drink mix	1 (454 g)
1¼ cups powdered sugar	310 ml

1. Combine all ingredients and store in airtight container.
2. To serve, use ¼ cup (60 ml) cocoa mix per cup of hot water.

Lemonade Tea

2 family-size tea bags	**2**
½ cup sugar	**125 ml**
1 (12 ounce) can frozen lemonade	**1 (340 g)**
1 quart ginger ale, chilled	**1 L**

1. Steep tea in 3 quarts (3 L) water and mix with sugar and lemonade.
2. Add ginger ale just before serving.

Victorian Iced Tea

4 individual tea bags	**4**
4 cups boiling water	**1 L**
1 (11 ounce) can frozen cranberry-raspberry	
juice concentrate, thawed	**1 (312 g)**
4 cups cold water	**1 L**

1. Place tea bags in teapot and add boiling water. Cover and steep for 5 minutes. Remove and discard tea bags. Refrigerate tea.
2. Just before serving, combine cranberry-raspberry concentrate and cold water in 2½-quart (2.5 L) pitcher. Stir in tea and serve with ic

Praline Coffee

3 cups hot brewed coffee	**750 ml**
¾ cup half-and-half cream	**180 ml**
¾ cup packed light brown sugar	**180 ml**
2 tablespoons butter	**30 ml**
¾ cup praline liqueur	**180 ml**

1. Cook coffee, cream and brown sugar in large saucepan over medium heat, stirring constantly. Do not boil.
2. Stir in liqueur and serve with sweetened whipped cream.

Strawberry Smoothie

2 medium bananas, peeled, sliced	**2**
1 pint fresh strawberries, washed, quartered	**500 ml**
1 (8 ounce) container strawberry yogurt	**1 (228 g)**
¼ cup orange juice	**60 ml**

1. Place all ingredients in blender. Process until smooth.
2. Serve as is or over crushed ice.

Kahlua Frosty

1 cup kahlua	250 ml
1 pint vanilla ice cream	500 ml
1 cup half-and-half cream	250 ml
⅛ teaspoon almond extract	.5 ml
1⅔ cups crushed ice	410 ml

1. Combine all ingredients in blender. Blend until smooth.
2. Serve immediately.

Kids' Cherry Sparkler

2 (6 ounce) jars red maraschino cherries, drained	2 (170 g)
2 (6 ounce) jars green maraschino cherries, drained	2 (170 g)
½ gallon distilled water	2 L
1 (2 liter) bottle cherry 7-UP, chilled	1 (2 L)

1. Place 1 red or green cherry in each compartment of 4 ice cube trays. Fill trays with distilled water and freeze for 8 hours.
2. Serve soft drink over ice cubes.

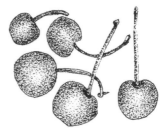

Pink Fizz

3 (6 ounce) cans frozen pink lemonade concentrate, undiluted	3 (170 g)
1 (750 ml) bottle pink sparkling wine	750 ml
3 (2 liter) bottles lemon-lime carbonated beverage, divided, chilled	3 (2 L)

1. Stir lemonade concentrate, wine and 2 bottles carbonated beverage in airtight container, cover and freeze 8 hours or until firm.
2. Let stand at room temperature 10 minutes and place in punch bowl. Add remaining bottle carbonated beverage and stir until slushy.

Wine Punch

2 (12 ounce) cans frozen limeade concentrate	2 (340 g)
4 limeade cans white wine, chilled	4
2 quarts ginger ale, chilled	2 L
Lime slices	

1. Combine limeade, white wine and ginger ale in punch bowl.
2. Serve with ice ring and lime slices.

Apple Party-Punch

3 cups sparkling apple cider	**750 ml**
2 cups apple juice	**500 ml**
1 cup pineapple juice	**250 ml**
½ cup brandy (optional)	**125 ml**

1. Combine all ingredients and freeze 8 hours.
2. Remove punch from freezer 30 minutes before serving. Place in small punch bowl and break into chunks. Stir until slushy.

★

Sparkling Punch

6 oranges, unpeeled, thinly sliced	**6**
1 cup sugar	**250 ml**
2 (750 ml) bottles dry white wine	**750 ml**
3 (750 ml) bottles sparkling wine, chilled	**750 ml**

1. Place orange slices in large non-metallic container and sprinkle with sugar.
2. Add white wine, cover and chill at least 8 hours.
3. Stir in sparkling wine.

Champagne Punch

1 (fifth) dry white wine, chilled	1 (800 ml)
1 cup apricot brandy	250 ml
1 cup triple sec	250 ml
2 bottles dry champagne, chilled	2
2 quarts club soda	2 L

1. In large pitcher, combine white wine, apricot brandy and triple sec. Cover and chill until ready to use.
2. At serving time, add champagne and club soda, stir to blend and pour punch into bowl.
3. Add ice ring to punch bowl.

Banana-Mango Smoothie

1 cup peeled, cubed, ripe mango	250 ml
1 ripe banana, sliced	1
⅔ cup milk	160 ml
1 teaspoon honey	5 ml
¼ teaspoon vanilla extract	1 ml

1. Arrange mango cubes in single layer on baking sheet and freeze until firm, about 1 hour.
2. Combine frozen mango, banana, milk, honey and vanilla and pour into blender.
3. Process until smooth.

Tropical Smoothie

1½ heaping cups peeled, seeded ripe papaya	375 ml
1 very ripe large banana	1
1½ heaping cups ripe cantaloupe, cut into chunks	375 ml
1 (6 ounce) carton coconut cream pie yogurt	1 (170 g)
¼ cup milk	60 ml

1. Cut papaya into chunks. Place all ingredients in a blender and puree until smooth.
2. Pour into glasses and serve immediately.

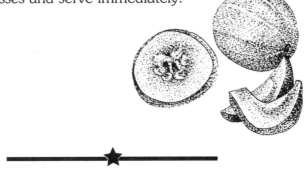

★

Amaretto

3 cups sugar	750 ml
2¼ cups water	560 ml
1 pint vodka	500 ml
3 tablespoons almond extract	45 ml
1 tablespoon vanilla (not the imitation)	15 ml

1. Combine sugar and water in large pan. Bring mixture to a boil and reduce heat. Simmer 5 minutes, stirring occasionally. Remove from stove.
2. Add vodka, almond extract and vanilla and stir to mix. Store in airtight jar.

Kahula

3 cups hot water	750 ml
1 cup instant coffee granules	250 ml
4 cups sugar	1 L
1 quart vodka	1 L
1 vanilla bean, split	1

1. In large saucepan, combine hot water, coffee granules and sugar and mix well. Bring to boil and boil 2 minutes. Cool.
2. Add vodka and vanilla bean. Pour into bottle or jar and let set for 30 days before serving. Shake occasionally. (If you happen to have some Mexican vanilla, you can make "instant" Kahula by using 3 tablespoons (45 ml) Mexican vanilla instead of vanilla bean – and no waiting 30 days.)

Sweet Orange Fluff

1¾ cups milk	430 ml
½ pint vanilla ice cream	250 ml
⅓ cup frozen orange juice concentrate	80 ml
1 teaspoon non-dairy creamer	5 ml

1. In blender, combine all ingredients. Blend until smooth.

BREADS, BRUNCH
&
BREAKFAST

Cheesy Herb Bread

1 loaf French bread	1
½ teaspoon garlic powder	2 ml
1 teaspoon marjoram leaves	5 ml
1 tablespoon dried parsley leaves	15 ml
½ cup (1 stick) butter, softened	125 ml
1 cup parmesan cheese	250 ml

1. Slice bread into 1-inch (2.5 cm) slices. Combine garlic, marjoram, parsley and butter. Spread mixture on bread slices and sprinkle with cheese.
2. Wrap in foil and bake at 375° (190° C) for 20 minutes. Unwrap and bake 5 more minutes.

Cheddar Butter Toast

½ cup (1 stick) butter, softened	125 ml
1¼ cups shredded cheddar cheese	310 ml
1 teaspoon worcestershire sauce	5 ml
¼ teaspoon garlic powder	1 ml
Thick sliced bread	

1. Combine all ingredients. Spread on thick sliced bread. Turn on broiler to toast, turn off broiler and leave in oven about 15 minutes.

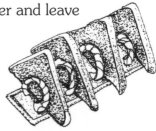

Crispy Herb Bread

1½ teaspoons basil	7 ml
1 teaspoon rosemary	5 ml
½ teaspoon thyme	2 ml
¾ cup (1½ sticks) butter, melted	180 ml
1 package hot dog buns	1

1. Combine basil, rosemary, thyme and butter and let stand several hours at room temperature. Spread on buns and cut into strips.
2. Bake at 300° (149° C) for 15 to 20 minutes or until crisp.

Crunchy Bread Sticks

1 package hot dog buns	1
1 cup (2 sticks) butter, melted	250 ml
Garlic powder	
Paprika	

1. Take each half bun and slice in half lengthwise. Use pastry brush to butter all bread sticks and sprinkle light amount of garlic powder and a couple of sprinkles of paprika.
2. Place on cookie sheet and bake at 225° (107° C) for about 45 minutes.

This is an all-time favorite of our family.
I keep these made up in the freezer.
We have served these several times at our
Cancer Society luncheons and everybody loves them.

Garlic Toast

1 loaf French bread	1
1 tablespoon garlic powder	15 ml
2 tablespoons dried parsley flakes	30 ml
½ cup (1 stick) butter, melted	125 ml
1 cup parmesan cheese	250 ml

1. Slice bread into 1-inch (2.5 cm) slices diagonally. In small bowl combine rest of ingredients except cheese and mix well. Use brush to spread mixture on bread slices and sprinkle with parmesan cheese.
2. Place on cookie sheet and bake at 225° (107° C) for about 1 hour.

Mozzarella Loaf

1 (12 inch) loaf French bread	1 (30 cm)
12 slices mozzarella cheese	12
¼ cup grated parmesan cheese	60 ml
6 tablespoons (¾ stick) butter, softened	90 ml
½ teaspoon garlic salt	2 ml

1. Cut loaf into 1-inch (2.5 cm) thick slices. Place slices of mozzarella between bread slices.
2. Combine parmesan cheese, butter and garlic salt. Spread on each slice of bread. Reshape loaf, press firmly together and brush remaining butter mixture on outside of loaf.
3. Bake at 375° (190° C) for 8 to 10 minutes.

Parmesan Bread Deluxe

1 loaf Italian bread	1
½ cup refrigerated creamy Caesar dressing	125 ml
⅓ cup grated parmesan cheese	80 ml
3 tablespoons finely chopped green onions	45 ml

1. Cut 24 (½ inch) (1 cm) thick slices from bread. Reserve remaining bread for other use.
2. In small bowl, combine dressing, cheese and onion. Spread 1 teaspoon (5 ml) dressing mixture on each bread slice.
3. Place bread on baking sheet. Broil 4 inches (10 cm) from heat until golden brown. Serve warm.

Chile Bread

1 loaf Italian bread, unsliced	1
½ cup (1 stick) butter, melted	125 ml
1 (4 ounce) can diced green chilies, drained	1 (115 g)
¾ cup grated Monterey Jack cheese	180 ml

1. Slice bread almost through. Combine melted butter, chilies and cheese. Spread between bread slices.
2. Cover loaf with foil.
3. Bake at 350° (176° C) for 15 minutes.

Ranch French Bread

½ cup (1 stick) butter, softened	125 ml
1 tablespoon ranch-style dressing mix	15 ml
1 loaf French bread	1

1. Cut loaf in half horizontally. Blend butter and dressing mix.
2. Spread butter mixture on bread. Wrap bread in foil.
3. Bake at 350° (176° C) for 15 minutes.

Poppy Seed Bread

3¾ cups biscuit mix	930 ml
1½ cups shredded cheddar cheese	375 ml
1 tablespoon poppy seeds	15 ml
1 egg, beaten	1
1½ cups milk	375 ml

1. Combine all ingredients and beat vigorously for 1 minute. Pour into greased loaf pan.
2. Bake at 350° (176° C) for 50 to 60 minutes. Test for doneness with toothpick. Remove from pan and cool before slicing.

Quick Pumpkin Bread

1 (16 ounce) package pound cake mix	1 (454 g)
1 cup canned pumpkin	250 ml
2 eggs	2
⅓ cup milk	80 ml
1 teaspoon allspice	5 ml

1. With mixer, beat all ingredients and blend well. Pour into greased, floured 9 x 5-inch (23 x 13 cm) loaf pan.
2. Bake at 350° (176° C) for 1 hour. Use toothpick to check to make sure bread is done.
3. Cool and turn onto cooling rack.

Butter Rolls

2 cups biscuit mix	**500 ml**
1 (8 ounce) carton sour cream	**1 (228 g)**
½ cup (1 stick) butter, melted	**125 ml**

1. Combine all ingredients and mix well. Spoon into greased muffin tins and fill only half full.
2. Bake at 400° (204° C) for 12 to 14 minutes or lightly brown.

Cheddar Cheese Loaf

3¾ cups biscuit mix	**930 ml**
¾ cup shredded sharp cheddar cheese	**180 ml**
1½ cups milk	**375 ml**
2 small eggs	**2**
⅛ teaspoon ground red pepper	**.5 ml**

1. Combine biscuit mix and cheese. Add milk, eggs and pepper and stir 2 minutes or until blended.
2. Spoon into 9 x 5-inch (23 x 13 cm) sprayed loaf pan.
3. Bake at 350° (176° C) for 45 minutes. Cool before slicing.

Popovers

2 cups flour	500 ml
1 teaspoon salt	5 ml
6 eggs, beaten	6
2 cups milk	500 ml
Butter	

1. Combine flour and salt in bowl. Add eggs and milk and mix. Add dry ingredients and mix well. (The batter will be like heavy cream.)
2. Coat popover pans with butter and heat in oven. Fill each cup half full.
3. Bake at 425° (218° C) for 20 minutes. Reduce heat to 375° (190° C) and bake 25 more minutes. Serve immediately.

Cream Biscuits

2 cups flour	500 ml
3 teaspoons baking powder	15 ml
½ teaspoon salt	2 ml
1 (8 ounce) carton whipping cream	1 (228 g)

1. Combine flour, baking powder and salt. In mixing bowl, beat whipping cream only until it holds a shape. Combine flour mixture and cream and mix with fork.
2. Put dough on lightly floured board and knead it for about 1 minute. Pat dough to ¾-inch (2 cm) thickness. Cut out biscuits with small biscuit cutter.
3. Place on baking sheet and bake at 375° (190° C) for about 12 minutes or until light brown.

Lickety-Split Biscuits

2 cups self-rising flour	500 ml
4 tablespoons mayonnaise	60 ml
1 cup milk	250 ml

1. Mix all ingredients and drop by spoonfuls on cookie sheet.
2. Bake at 425° (218° C) until biscuits are golden brown.

Refrigerator Biscuits

1 (8 ounce) package cream cheese, softened	1 (228 g)
½ cup (1 stick) butter, softened	125 ml
1 cup self-rising flour	250 ml

1. Beat cream cheese and butter at medium speed with mixer for 2 minutes. Gradually add flour, beating at low speed, just until blended.
2. Spoon dough into miniature muffin pans, filling two-thirds full, or refrigerate dough for up to 3 days.
3. Bake at 375° (190° C) for 15 minutes or until golden brown.

Sausage Biscuits

1 (8 ounce) package grated cheddar cheese	1 (228 g)
1 pound hot bulk pork sausage	454 g
2 cup biscuit mix	500 ml

1. Combine all three ingredients. Drop on ungreased cookie sheet.
2. Bake at 400° (204° C) until light brown. Serve hot.

Sour Cream Biscuits

2 cups plus	500 ml+
1 tablespoon flour	15 ml
3 teaspoons baking powder	15 ml
½ teaspoon baking soda	2 ml
½ cup shortening	125 ml
1 (8 ounce) carton sour cream	1 (228 g)

1. Combine dry ingredients, add a little salt and cut in shortening.
2. Gradually add sour cream and mix lightly. Turn on lightly floured board and knead a few times. Roll to ½ inch (1 cm) thick. Cut with biscuit cutter and place on greased baking sheet.
3. Bake at 400° (204° C) for 15 minutes or until light brown.

Spicy Cornbread Twists

3 tablespoons (⅓ stick) butter	45 ml
⅓ cup cornmeal	80 ml
¼ teaspoon red pepper	1 ml
1 (11 ounce) can refrigerated soft breadsticks	1 (312 g)

1. Place butter in pie plate and melt in oven. Remove from oven.
2. On piece of wax paper, mix cornmeal and red pepper. Roll breadsticks in butter and in cornmeal mixture.
3. Twist breadsticks as label directs and place on cookie sheet. Bake at 350° (176° C) 15 to 18 minutes.

Hush Puppies

1¼ cups yellow cornmeal	310 ml
1 teaspoon salt	5 ml
1 cup boiling water	250 ml
½ onion, finely minced	½
1 eggs, beaten	1

1. Combine cornmeal and salt. Bring water to boiling in saucepan, add meal and salt and stir constantly. Cook until smooth and thick and cool.
2. Add onion and egg and mix thoroughly.
3. Form into small balls, roll in flour and deep fry.

Cheddar Cornbread

2 (8½ ounce) packages cornbread-muffin mix	2 (242 g)
2 eggs, beaten	2
½ cup milk	125 ml
½ cup plain yogurt	125 ml
1 (15 ounce) can cream-style corn	1 (438 g)
½ cup shredded cheddar cheese	125 ml

1. In bowl, combine cornbread mix, eggs, milk and yogurt until blended.
2. Stir in corn and cheese. Pour into greased 9 x 13-inch (23 x 33 cm) baking dish.
3. Bake at 400° (204° C) for 18 to 20 minutes or until light brown.

Souper-Sausage Cornbread

1 (10 ounce) can golden corn soup	1 (284 g)
2 eggs	2
¼ cup milk	60 ml
2 (6 ounce) packages corn muffin mix	2 (170 g)
¼ pound pork sausage, cooked, drained, crumbled	115 g

1. In bowl, combine soup, eggs and milk. Stir in muffin mix just until blended.
2. Fold in sausage. Spoon mixture into greased 9 x 13-inch (23 x 33 cm) baking pan.
3. Bake at 400° (204° C) for about 20 minutes or until light brown.

Fried Cornbread

2 cups cornmeal	500 ml
1¼ teaspoons salt	6 ml
½ teaspoon sugar	2 ml
1 teaspoon baking powder	5 ml
Oil	

1. Combine dry ingredients and add just enough boiling water to form a fairly stiff dough.
2. To fry, heat a little oil in skillet. Take heaping tablespoon dough and place in skillet. Pat down with back of spoon so it can be turned over and fried on the top side. If the last few spoons of cornbread get a little dry, add just a drip or two more water.
3. Brown on both sides and serve immediately.

Sour Cream Cornbread

1 cup self-rising cornmeal	250 ml
1 (8 ounce) can cream-style corn	1 (228 g)
1 (8 ounce) carton sour cream	1 (228 g)
3 large eggs, lightly beaten	3
¼ cup oil	60 ml

1. Heat lightly greased 8-inch (20 cm) cast-iron skillet in at 400° (204° C).
2. Combine all ingredients and stir just until moist. Remove prepared skillet from oven and spoon batter into hot skillet.
3. Bake at 400° (204° C) for 20 minutes or until golden.

Cheese Muffins

3¾ cups buttermilk biscuit mix	930 ml
1¼ cups grated cheddar cheese	310 ml
1 egg, beaten	1
1¼ cups milk	310 ml
Dash chili powder	

1. In large bowl, combine all ingredients and beat vigorously by hand.
2. Pour into greased muffin tins.
3. Bake at 325° (163° C) for 35 minutes.

Salad Muffins

⅓ **cup sugar**	**80 ml**
⅓ **cup oil**	**80 ml**
¾ **cup milk**	**180 ml**
2 eggs	**2**
2 cups biscuit mix	**500 ml**

1. In mixing bowl, combine sugar, oil and milk. Beat in eggs and biscuit mix.
2. Mix well; mixture will be a little lumpy. Pour into greased muffin tins two-thirds full.
3. Bake at 400° (204° C) for about 10 minutes or until light brown.

Mayo Muffins

1¼ **cups self-rising flour**	**310 ml**
3 tablespoons mayonnaise	**45 ml**
1 cup whole milk	**250 ml**

1. Mix all ingredients and spoon into greased muffin tins.
2. Bake at 375° (190° C) for 20 minutes or until light brown.

Ginger-Raisin Muffins

1 (18 ounce) box gingerbread mix	1 (520 g)
1¼ cups lukewarm water	310 ml
1 egg	1
2 (1½ ounce) boxes seedless raisins	2 (42 g)

1. Combine gingerbread mix, water and egg and mix well. Stir in raisins.
2. Pour into greased muffin tins filled half full.
3. Bake at 350° (176° C) for 20 minutes or when tested with toothpick.

Kids' Corn Dog Muffins

2 (6 ounce) corn bread muffin mix	2 (170 g)
2 tablespoons brown sugar	30 ml
2 eggs	2
1 cup milk	250 ml
1 (8 ounce) can whole kernel corn, drained	1 (228 g)
5 hot dogs, chopped	5

1. In bowl, combine corn bread mix and brown sugar. Combine eggs and milk and stir into dry ingredients. Stir in corn and hot dogs. (Batter will be thin.)
2. Fill greased muffin cups ¾ full. Bake at 400° (204° C) for 16 to 18 minutes or until golden brown.

Orange-French Toast

1 egg, beaten	1
½ cup orange juice	125 ml
5 slices raisin bread	5
1 cup crushed graham crackers	250 ml
2 tablespoons butter	30 ml

1. Combine egg and orange juice. Dip bread in mixture and then in crumbs.
2. Fry in butter until brown.

French Toast

4 eggs	4
1 cup whipping cream	250 ml
2 thick slices bread, cut into 3 strips	2
Powdered sugar	

1. Place a little oil in skillet. Beat eggs, cream and a pinch of salt. Dip bread into batter allowing batter to soak. Fry bread in skillet until brown, turn and fry on other side. Transfer to cookie sheet.
2. Bake at 325° (163° C) for about 4 minutes or until puffed.
3. Sprinkle with powdered sugar.

Breakfast Bake

1 pound hot sausage, cooked, crumbled	454 g
1 cup grated cheddar cheese	250 ml
1 cup biscuit mix	250 ml
5 eggs, slightly beaten	5
2 cups milk	500 ml

1. Place cooked, crumbled sausage in sprayed 9 x 13-inch (23 x 33 cm) baking dish. Sprinkle with cheese.
2. In mixing bowl, combine biscuit mix, a little salt and eggs and beat well. Add milk and stir until fairly smooth. Pour over sausage mixture.
3. Bake covered at 350° (176° C) for 35 minutes. You can mix this up the night before cooking and refrigerate. To cook the next morning, add 5 minutes to cooking time.

This is a favorite of ours for over-night guests or special enough for Christmas morning.

Christmas Breakfast

12 to 14 eggs, slightly beaten	12 to 14
1 pound sausage, cooked, drained, crumbled	454 g
2 cups whole milk	500 ml
1½ cups grated cheddar cheese	375 ml
1 (5.5 ounce) box seasoned croutons	1 (156 g)

1. Mix all ingredients and pour into 9 x 13-inch (23 x 33 cm) baking dish.
2. Bake covered at 350° (176° C) for 40 minutes. Let rest for about 10 minutes before serving.

Bacon-Sour Cream Omelet

2 eggs	**2**
2 strips bacon, fried, drained, crumbled	**2**
⅓ cup sour cream	**80 ml**
3 green onions, chopped	**3**
1 tablespoon butter	**15 ml**

1. Using fork, beat eggs with 1 tablespoon (15 ml) water. Combine bacon and sour cream. Saute onions in remaining bacon drippings. Mix with bacon-sour cream.
2. Melt butter in omelet pan. Pour in egg mixture and cook. When omelet is set, spoon sour cream mixture along center and fold omelet onto warm plate.

Huevos Rancheros

8 eggs	**8**
3 tablespoons oil	**45 ml**
4 corn tortillas	**4**
1 cup grated Monterrey Jack cheese	**250 ml**
Enchilada Sauce	

1. Lightly fry 2 eggs at a time.
2. Fry tortillas in hot oil and drain. Place 2 eggs on tortilla. Repeat process for other servings.
3. Pour enchilada sauce over eggs, top with cheese and serve.

Sunrise Eggs

6 eggs	6
2 cups milk	500 ml
1 pound sausage, cooked, browned	454 ml
¾ cup grated processed cheese	180 ml
6 slices white bread, trimmed, cubed	6

1. Beat eggs and add milk, sausage and cheese. Pour over bread and mix well.
2. Pour into greased 9 x 13-inch (23 x 33 cm) baking pan and cover with foil.
3. Bake at 350° (176° C) for 20 minutes. Remove foil and turn oven up to 375° (190° C) and bake for another 10 minutes.

Mexican-Breakfast Eggs

¼ cup (½ stick) butter	60 ml
9 eggs	9
3 tablespoons milk	45 ml
5 tablespoons salsa	90 ml
1 cup crushed tortilla chips	250 ml

1. Melt butter in skillet. In bowl, beat eggs and add milk and salsa.
2. Pour into skillet and stir until eggs are lightly cooked.
3. Stir in tortilla chips. Serve hot.

Chiffon-Cheese Souffle

12 slices white bread, crust trimmed	12
2 (5 ounce) jars Old English cheese spread, softened	2 (142 g)
6 eggs, beaten	6
3 cups milk	750 ml
¾ cup (1½ sticks) butter, melted	180 ml

1. Spray 9 x 13-inch (23 x 33 cm) baking dish with non-stick vegetable coating. Cut each slice bread into 4 triangles. Place dab (with a knife) cheese on each triangle and place triangles evenly in layers in baking dish. You could certainly make this in souffle dish if you have one.
2. Combine eggs, milk, butter and a little salt and pepper. Pour over layers. Cover and chill 8 hours.
3. Remove from refrigerator 10 to 15 minutes before baking. Bake at 350° (176° C) uncovered for 1 hour.

Green Chili Squares

2 cups chopped green chilies	500 ml
1 (8 ounce) package shredded sharp cheddar cheese	1 (228 g)
8 eggs, beaten	8
Salt and pepper	
½ cup half-and-half cream	125 ml

1. Place green chilies on bottom of 9 x 13-inch (23 x 33 cm) baking pan. Cover with cheese.
2. Combine eggs, salt, pepper and cream. Pour over chilies and cheese.
3. Bake at 350° (176° C) for 30 minutes. Let rest at room temperature for a few minutes before cutting into squares.

Pineapple-Cheese Casserole

2 (20 ounce) cans unsweetened pineapple chunks, drained	2 (570 g)
1 cup sugar, 5 tablespoons flour	250 ml
	75 ml
1½ cups grated cheddar cheese	375 ml
1 stack buttery crackers, crushed	1
½ cup (1 stick) butter, melted	125 ml

1. Grease 9 x 13-inch (23 x 33 cm) baking dish and layer ingredients in following order: pineapple, sugar-flour mixture, grated cheese and cracker crumbs.
2. Drizzle butter over casserole.
3. Bake at 350° (176° C) for 25 minutes or until bubbly.

This is really a different kind of recipe – but so good.
It can be served at brunch and it's great
with sandwiches at lunch.

Crabmeat Quiche

3 eggs, beaten	3
1 (8 ounce) carton sour cream	1 (228 g)
1 (6 ounce) can crabmeat, rinsed	1 (170 g)
½ cup grated Swiss cheese	125 ml
1 (9 inch) pie shell	1 (240 g)

1. In bowl, combine eggs and sour cream. Blend in crabmeat and cheese and add a little garlic salt and pepper.
2. Pour into 9-inch (23 cm) unbaked pie shell.
3. Bake at 350° (176° C) for 35 minutes.

Apricot Casserole

4 (15 ounce) cans apricot halves, drained, divided	4 (438 g)
1 (16 ounce) box light brown sugar, divided	1 (454 g)
1 stack buttery crackers, crumbled, divided	1
½ cup (1 stick) butter, sliced, divided	125 ml

1. Grease 9 x 13-inch (23 x 33 cm) baking dish and line bottom with 2 cans drained apricots.
2. Sprinkle half brown sugar and half cracker crumbs over apricots. Dot with half butter. Repeat layers.
3. Bake at 300° (149° C) for 1 hour.

Cinnamon Souffle

1 loaf cinnamon raisin bread	1
1 (20 ounce) can crushed pineapple with juice	1 (570 g)
1 cup (2 sticks) butter, melted	250 ml
½ cup sugar	125 ml
5 eggs, slightly beaten	5

1. Slice very thin amount of crusts off. Tear bread into small pieces and place in buttered 9 x 13-inch (23 x 33 cm) baking dish.
2. Pour pineapple and juice over bread and set aside. Cream butter and sugar. Add eggs to creamed mixture and mix well.
3. Pour creamed mixture over bread and pineapple. Bake at 350° (176° C) uncovered for 40 minutes. (Add ½ cup (125 ml) chopped pecans if you like.)

Light, Crispy Waffles

2 cups biscuit mix	500 ml
1 egg	1
½ cup oil	125 ml
1⅓ cups club soda	330 ml

1. Preheat waffle iron. Combine all ingredients in mixing bowl and stir by hand. Pour just enough batter to cover waffle iron.
2. To have waffles for "company weekend", make up all waffles. Freeze separately on cookie sheet, place in large baggies. Heat, at 350° (176° C) for about 10 minutes.

Melon Boats

2 cantaloupes, chilled	2
4 cups red and green seedless grapes, chilled	1 L
1 cup mayonnaise	250 ml
⅓ cup frozen concentrated orange juice with juice	80 ml

1. Prepare each melon in 6 lengthwise sections and remove seeds and peel. Place on separate salad plates on lettuce leaves. Heap grapes over and around cantaloupe slices.
2. Combine mayonnaise and juice concentrate and mix well. Ladle over fruit.

Curried-Fruit Medley

1 (29 ounce) can sliced peaches	1 (828 g)
2 (15 ounce) cans pineapple chunks	2 (438 g)
1 (10 ounce) jar maraschino cherries	1 (284 g)
1 cup packed brown sugar	250 ml
1 teaspoon curry powder	5 ml
¼ cup (½ stick) butter, cut into pieces	60 ml

1. Drain fruit and place in 9 x 13-inch (23 x 33 cm) baking dish.
2. Combine brown sugar and curry and stir well. Sprinkle over fruit and dot with butter.
3. Bake covered at 350° (176° C) for 30 minutes or until thoroughly heated.

Treasure-Filled Apples

6 medium, tart apples	6
½ cup sugar	125 ml
¼ cup red hot candies	60 ml
¼ teaspoon ground cinnamon	60 ml

1. Cut tops off apples and set tops aside. Core apples to within ½ inch (1 cm) of bottom. Place in greased 8-inch (20 cm) baking dish.
2. In bowl, combine sugar, candies and cinnamon and spoon 2 tablespoons (30 ml) into each apple. Replace tops. Spoon any remaining sugar mixture over apples.
3. Bake uncovered at 350° (176° C) for 30 to 35 minutes or until apples are tender. Baste occasionally.

Ranch Sausage-Grits

1 cup quick-cooking grits	250 ml
1 pound pork sausage	454 g
1 onion, chopped	1
1 cup salsa	250 ml
1 (8 ounce) package shredded cheddar cheese, divided	1 (228 g)

1. Cook grits according to directions and set aside. Cook and brown sausage and onion and drain. Combine grits, sausage mixture, salsa and half cheese. Spoon into greased 2-quart (2 L) baking dish.
2. Bake at 350° (176° C) for 15 minutes. Remove from oven and add remaining cheese on top of casserole.
3. Bake another 10 minutes. Serve hot.

Baked Grits

2 cups quick grits	500 ml
4 cups water	1 L
2 cups milk	500 ml
¾ cup (1½ sticks) butter	180 ml
4 eggs, beaten	4

1. Stir grits in water over medium heat for about 5 minutes. Add milk and butter, cover and cook another 10 minutes.
2. Remove from heat and add beaten eggs.
3. Pour in buttered casserole and bake covered at 350° (176° C) for 30 minutes.

Gingered-Cream Spread

1 (8 ounce) package cream cheese, softened	1 (228 g)
½ cup (1 stick) unsalted butter, softened	125 ml
2 tablespoons milk	30 ml
3 tablespoons finely chopped crystallized ginger	45 ml

1. Combine all ingredients in mixing bowl. Beat until creamy
2. Spread on favorite fruit or nut breads.

Homemade Egg Substitute

6 egg whites	6
¼ cup instant nonfat dry milk powder	60 ml
2 teaspoons water	10 ml
2 teaspoons oil	10 ml
¼ teaspoon ground turmeric	1 ml

1. Combine all ingredients in electric blender and process 30 seconds.
2. Refrigerate. One egg is the equivalent to ¼ cup (60 ml).

Blueberry Coffee Cake

1 (16 ounce) package blueberry muffin mix	1 (454 g)
⅓ cup sour cream	80 ml
1 egg	1
⅔ cup powdered sugar	160 ml
1 tablespoon water	15 ml

1. Stir muffin mix, sour cream, egg and ½ cup (125 ml) water. Rinse blueberries and gently fold into batter. Pour into sprayed 7 x 11-inch (18 x 28 cm) baking dish.
2. Bake at 400° (204° C) for about 25 minutes and cool.
3. Mix powdered sugar and 1 tablespoon (15 ml) water and drizzle over coffee cake.

Pineapple Coffee Cake

1 (18 ounce) box butter cake mix	1 (520 g)
½ cup oil	125 ml
4 eggs, slightly beaten	4
1 (20 ounce) can pineapple pie filling	1 (570 g)

1. In mixing bowl, combine cake mix, oil and eggs and beat well.
2. Pour batter into greased, floured 9 x 13-inch (23 x 33 cm) baking pan. Bake at 350° (176° C) for 45 to 50 minutes. Test with toothpick to make sure cake is done.
3. With knife, punch holes in cake about 2 inches (5 cm) apart. Spread pineapple pie filling over cake while cake is still hot.

SOUPS, SALADS
&
SANDWICHES

Spicy Tomato Soup

2 (10 ounce) cans tomato soup	2 (284 g)
1 (16 ounce) can Mexican stewed tomatoes	1 (454 g)
Sour cream	
½ pound bacon, fried, drained, crumbled	228 g

1. In saucepan, combine soup and stewed tomatoes and heat.
2. To serve, place dollop of sour cream on each bowl of soup and sprinkle crumbled bacon over sour cream.

Beef-Noodle Soup

1 pound lean ground beef	454 g
1 (46 ounce) can cocktail vegetable juice	1 (1.3 kg)
1 (1 ounce) envelope onion soup mix	1 (28 g)
1 (3 ounce) package beef ramen noodles	1 (85 g)
1 (16 ounce) package frozen mixed vegetables	1 (454 g)

1. In large saucepan, cook beef over medium heat until no longer pink and drain. Stir in vegetable juice, soup mix, noodle seasoning packet and mixed vegetables and bring to boil.
2. Reduce heat and simmer, uncovered, for 6 minutes or until vegetables are tender.
3. Return to boil and stir in noodles. Cook for 3 minutes or until noodles are tender. Serve hot.

Broccoli-Wild Rice Soup

1 (6 ounce) package chicken-flavored wild rice mix	**1 (170 g)**
1 (10 ounce) package frozen chopped broccoli, thawed	**1 (284 g)**
2 teaspoons dried minced onion	**10 ml**
1 (10 ounce) can cream of chicken soup	**1 (284 g)**
1 (8 ounce) package cream cheese, cubed	**1 (228 g)**

1. In large saucepan, combine rice, rice seasoning packet and 6 cups (1.5 L) water. Bring to boil, reduce heat, cover and simmer for 10 minutes, stirring once.
2. Stir in broccoli and onion and simmer 5 minutes.
3. Stir in soup and cream cheese. Cook and stir until cheese melts.

This is a hardy, delicious soup that is full of flavor.

Warm-Your-Soul Soup

3 (15 ounce) cans chicken broth	**3 (438 g)**
1 (10 ounce) can Italian-stewed tomatoes with liquid	**1 (284 g)**
½ cup onion, chopped	**125 ml**
¾ cup chopped celery	**180 ml**
½ (12 ounce) box fettuccine	**½ (340 g)**

1. In large soup kettle, combine chicken broth, tomatoes, onion and celery. Bring to boil and simmer until onion and celery are almost done.
2. Add pasta and cook according to package directions. Season with a little salt and pepper.

Great flavor – great soup!

Crab Bisque

1 (10 ounce) can cream of celery soup	1 (284 g)
1 (10 ounce) can pepper-pot soup	1 (284 g)
1 pint half-and-half cream	500 ml
1 (6 ounce) can crabmeat, drained	1 (170 g)
A scant ⅓ cup sherry	80 ml

1. Mix soups and half-and-half.
2. Shred crabmeat, add to soups and heat.
3. Just before serving, add sherry.

Clam Chowder

1 (10 ounce) can New England clam chowder	1 (284 g)
1 (10 ounce) can cream of celery soup	1 (284 g)
1 (10 ounce) can cream of potato soup	1 (284 g)
1 (6.5 ounce) can chopped clams	1 (184 g)
1 soup can milk	284 g

1. Combine all ingredients in saucepan.
2. Heat and stir.

Cream of Cauliflower Soup

1 onion, chopped	1
½ teaspoon garlic powder	2 ml
2 (14 ounce) cans chicken broth	2 (420 g)
1 large cauliflower, cut into small flowerets	1
1½ cups whipping cream	375 ml

1. Saute onion and garlic powder in 1 tablespoon (15 ml) butter. Stir in broth and bring to a boil. Add cauliflower and cook, stirring occasionally, 15 minutes or until tender.
2. Process soup in batches in blender until smooth and return to pan.
3. Stir in cream and add a little salt and white pepper. Cook over low heat, stirring often, until thoroughly heated.

Cream of Zucchini Soup

1 pound fresh zucchini, grated	454 g
1 onion, chopped	1
1 (15 ounce) can chicken broth	1 (438 g)
½ teaspoon sweet basil	2 ml
2 cups half-and-half cream	500 ml

1. In saucepan, combine zucchini, onion, broth, basil plus a little salt and pepper. Bring to a boil and simmer until soft. Pour into food processor and puree.
2. Gradually add ½ cup (125 ml) half-and-half and blend. Add ¼ teaspoon (60 ml) curry powder, if you like the curry flavor.
3. Return zucchini mixture to saucepan and add remaining half-and-half. Heat, but to not boil.

Creamy Butternut Soup

4 cups cooked, mashed butternut squash	**1 L**
2 (14 ounce) cans chicken broth	**2 (420 g)**
½ teaspoon sugar	**2 ml**
1 (8 ounce) carton whipping cream, divided	**1 (228 g)**
¼ teaspoon ground nutmeg	**1 ml**

1. In saucepan, combine mashed squash, broth, sugar and a little salt. Bring to a boil and gradually stir in half of whipping cream Cook until thoroughly heated.
2. Beat remaining whipping cream. When ready to serve, place dollop of whipped cream on soup and sprinkle of nutmeg.

Easy Potato Soup

1 (16 ounce) package frozen hash brown	
potatoes	**1 (454 g)**
1 cup chopped onion	**250 ml**
1 (14 ounce) can chicken broth	**1 (420 g)**
1 (10 ounce) can cream of celery soup,	**1 (284 g)**
1 (10 ounce) can cream of chicken soup	**1 (284 g)**
2 cups milk	**500 ml**

1. In large saucepan, combine potatoes, onion and 2 cups (500 ml) water and bring to a boil. Cover, reduce heat and simmer 30 minutes.
2. Stir in broth, soups and milk and heat thoroughly. (If you like, garnish with shredded cheddar cheese or diced, cooked ham.)

Navy Bean Soup

3 (15 ounce) cans navy beans with liquid	3 (438 g)
1 (14 ounce) can chicken broth	1 (420 g)
1 cup chopped ham	250 ml
1 large onion, chopped	1
½ teaspoon garlic powder	2 ml

1. In large saucepan, combine beans, broth, ham, onion and garlic powder. Add 1 cup (250 ml) water and bring to a boil. Simmer until onion is tender crisp.
2. Serve hot with cornbread.

★

Peanut Soup

2 (10 ounce) cans cream of chicken soup	2 (284 g)
2 soup cans milk	570 g
1¼ cups crunchy-style peanut butter	310 ml

1. In saucepan on medium heat, blend soup and milk.
2. Stir in peanut butter and heat until well blended.

Cold Cucumber Soup

3 medium cucumbers, peeled, seeded, cut into chunks	3
1 (14 ounce) can chicken broth, divided	1 (420 g)
1 (8 ounce) carton sour cream	1 (228 g)
3 tablespoons fresh chives, minced	45 ml
2 teaspoons fresh dill, minced	10 ml

1. In blender, combine cucumbers, 1 cup (250 ml) chicken broth and dash of salt. Cover and process until smooth. Transfer to medium bowl and stir in remaining chicken broth.
2. Whisk in sour cream, chives and dill. Cover and chill well before serving.
3. Garnish with dill sprig.

Chilled Squash Soup

2 pounds yellow squash, thinly sliced	1 kg
1 onion, chopped	1
1 (14 ounce) can chicken broth	1 (420 g)
1 (8 ounce) package cream cheese, softened	1 (228 g)
¼ teaspoon freshly ground pepper	1 ml

1. Combine squash, onion and broth in saucepan and bring to a boil. Cover, reduce heat and simmer 10 minutes or until tender; cool.
2. Spoon half of squash mixture and half cream cheese into blender. Process until smooth, stopping once to scrape down sides. Repeat procedure.
3. Stir in pepper and chill.

Avocado-Cream Soup

4 ripe avocados, peeled, diced	**4**
1½ cups whipping cream	**375 ml**
2 (14 ounce) cans chicken broth	**2 (420 g)**
1 teaspoon salt	**5 ml**
¼ cup dry sherry	**60 ml**

1. With blender, cream half avocados and half cream. Repeat with remaining avocados and cream.
2. Bring broth to a boil, reduce heat and stir in avocado puree. Add salt and sherry and chill thoroughly.
3. To serve, place in individual bowls and sprinkle a little paprika on top.

Asparagus Chiller

1 (10 ounce) can cream of asparagus soup	**1 (284 g)**
⅔ cup plain yogurt	**160 ml**
½ cup chopped cucumber	**125 ml**
2 tablespoons chopped red onion	**30 ml**

1. Blend soup, yogurt and 1 soup can (284 g) water. Add cucumber and onion.
2. Chill at least 4 hours and serve in chilled bowls.

Cold Strawberry Soup

2¼ cups strawberries	560 ml
⅓ cup sugar	80 ml
½ cup sour cream	125 ml
½ cup whipping cream	125 ml
½ cup light red wine	125 ml

1. Place strawberries and sugar in blender and puree. Pour into pitcher, stir in sour cream and whipping cream and blend well.
2. Add 1¼ cups (310 ml) water and red wine. Stir and chill.

Strawberry Soup

1½ cups fresh strawberries	375 ml
1 cup orange juice	250 ml
¼ cup honey	60 ml
½ cup sour cream	125 ml
½ cup white wine	125 ml

1. Combine all ingredients in blender and puree.
2. Chill thoroughly. Stir before serving.

Broccoli-Waldorf Salad

6 cups fresh broccoli florets	1.5 L
1 large red apple with peel, chopped	1
½ cup golden raisins	125 ml
½ cup chopped pecans	125 ml
½ cup prepared coleslaw dressing	125 ml

1. In large bowl, combine broccoli, apple, raisins and pecans.
2. Drizzle with the dressing and toss to coat. Refrigerate.
3. Serve in pretty crystal bowl.

Broccoli-Noodle Salad

1 cup silvered almonds, toasted	250 ml
1 cup sunflower seeds, toasted	250 ml
2 (3 ounce) packages chicken ramen noodles	2 (85 g)
1 (10 ounce) package broccoli slaw	1 (284 g)
1 (8 ounce) bottle Italian salad dressing	1 (228 g)

1. Toast almonds and sunflower seeds in oven at 275° (135° C) for about 10 minutes.
2. Break up ramen noodles and mix with slaw, almonds and sunflower seeds.
3. Toss with Italian salad dressing and chill.

Broccoli-Green Bean Salad

1 large bunch broccoli, cut into florets	1
2 (15 ounce) cans cut green beans, drained	2 (438 g)
1 bunch fresh green onions with tops, chopped	1
2 (6 ounce) jars marinated artichoke hearts, chopped, drained	2 (170 g)
1½ cups ranch-style dressing (with mayonnaise)	375 ml

1. Combine broccoli, green beans, onions and artichokes and mix well.
2. Add dressing, toss and chill 24 hours before serving.

Broccoli-Cauliflower Salad

1 small head cauliflower	1
3 stalks broccoli, 1 cup mayonnaise	3, 250 ml
1 tablespoon vinegar, 1 tablespoon sugar	15 ml
1 bunch fresh green onions with tops, chopped	1
8 ounces mozzarella cheese, cubed	228 g

1. Cut up cauliflower and broccoli into bite-size flowerets. Combine mayonnaise, vinegar and sugar.
2. Combine cauliflower, broccoli, mayonnaise mixture, onions and cheese. Add a little salt if you like. Toss and refrigerate.

Garlic-Green Beans

3 (15 ounce) cans whole green beans, drained   3 (438 g)
⅔ cup oil   160 ml
½ cup vinegar   125 ml
½ cup sugar   125 ml
5 buttons garlic, finely chopped   5

1. Place green beans in container with lid. Mix oil, vinegar, sugar and garlic and pour over beans. Sprinkle with a little salt and red pepper.
2. Chill overnight.

Summertime-Mushroom Salad

1 (8 ounce) package cream cheese, softened   1 (228 g)
½ cup mayonnaise   125 ml
½ teaspoon salt   2 ml
1 bunch fresh green onions with tops, chopped   1
4 cups fresh mushrooms, sliced   1 L

1. In mixing bowl, blend cream cheese, mayonnaise and salt.
2. Gently mix in onions and mushrooms. Chill and serve on lettuce leaf.

Winter Salad

1 (15 ounce) can cut green beans, drained	1 (438 g)
1 (15 ounce) can English peas, drained	1 (438 g)
1 (15 ounce) can whole kernel corn, drained	1 (438 g)
1 (15 ounce) can jalapeno black-eyed peas, drained	1 (438 g)
1 (8 ounce) bottle Italian dressing	1 (228 g)

1. Combine all vegetables in large bowl. (Add some chopped onion and chopped bell pepper if you like.)
2. Pour Italian dressing over vegetables.
3. Cover and refrigerate.

This is a great make-ahead salad and will stay fresh at least a week.

Marinated Black-Eyed Peas

3 (15 ounce) cans jalapeno black-eyed peas, drained	3 (438 g)
1 cup chopped celery	250 ml
1 bunch fresh green onions with tops, chopped	1
1 (4 ounce) jar pimentos, drained	1 (115 g)
1 (8 ounce) bottle Italian dressing	1 (228 g)

1. Mix all ingredients and chill.
2. Let rest several hours before serving.

Green Pea Salad

1 (16 ounce) bag frozen green peas	1 (454 g)
1 bunch fresh green onions with tops, chopped	1
½ cup chopped celery	125 ml
½ cup sweet pickle relish	125 ml
Mayonnaise	

1. Mix peas, onions, celery and relish.
2. Add enough mayonnaise to hold salad together and chill.

Sunflower Salad

2 apples, cored, chopped	2
1 cup seedless green grapes, halved	250 ml
½ cup chopped celery	125 ml
¾ cup chopped pecans	180 ml
⅓ cup mayonnaise	80 ml

1. Combine all ingredients and chill.

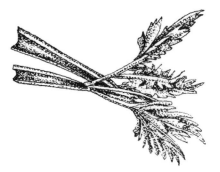

Avocado-Green Bean Salad

2 (15 ounce) cans French-cut green beans, drained	2 (438 g)
8 green onions with tops, chopped	8
¾ cup Italian salad dressing	180 ml
2 avocados	2
1 (8 ounce) can artichoke hearts, drained	1 (228 g)

1. Place green beans and onions in serving dish. Pour dressing over mixture and refrigerate several hours or overnight.
2. When ready to serve, chop avocados and artichoke hearts and stir in with beans and onions.

Cold Butter-Bean Salad

2 (10 ounce) packages frozen baby limas	2 (284 g)
1 (15 ounce) can shoe-peg corn, drained	1 (438 g)
1 bunch fresh green onions with tops, chopped	1
1 cup mayonnaise	250 ml
2 teaspoons ranch and salad dressing seasoning	10 ml

1. Cook beans according to directions and drain.
2. Add corn, onions, mayonnaise and seasoning, mix well and chill.

Nutty Green Salad

6 cups torn, mixed salad greens	1.5 L
1 medium zucchini, sliced	1
1 (8 ounce) can sliced water chestnuts, drained	1 (228 g)
½ cup peanuts	125 ml
⅓ cup Italian salad dressing	80 ml

1. Toss greens, zucchini, water chestnuts and peanuts.
2. When ready to serve, add salad dressing and toss.

Spinach-Apple Salad

1 (10 ounce) package fresh spinach	1 (284 g)
⅓ cup frozen orange juice concentrate, thawed	80 ml
¾ cup mayonnaise	180 ml
1 red apple	1
5 slices bacon, fried, crumbled	5

1. Tear spinach into small pieces.
2. Mix orange juice concentrate and mayonnaise.
3. When ready to serve, chop apple with peel and mix with spinach. Pour dressing over salad and top with bacon.

City Slicker Salad

2 (10 ounce) packages fresh spinach	**2 (284 g)**
1 quart fresh strawberries, halved	**1 L**
½ cup slivered almonds, toasted	**125 ml**
Poppy seed dressing	

1. Tear spinach into smaller pieces and add strawberries and almonds.
2. Refrigerate until ready to serve. Toss with poppy seed dressing.

Merry Berry Salad

1 (10 ounce) package mixed salad greens	**1 (284 g)**
2 apples, 1 red and 1 green, diced	**2**
1 cup shredded parmesan cheese	**250 ml**
½ cup dried cranberries	**125 ml**
½ cup slivered almonds, toasted	**125 ml**

1. In large salad bowl, toss greens, apples, cheese, cranberries and almonds.
2. Drizzle poppy seed dressing over salad and toss.

Green and Red Salad

4 cups torn mixed salad greens	1 L
3 fresh green onions with tops, chopped	3
2 medium red apples with peels, diced	2
1 cup fresh raspberries	250 ml
½ cup poppy seed dressing	125 ml

1. In bowl, toss salad greens, onions and fruit.
2. Drizzle with dressing and toss.

Marinated Corn Salad

3 (15 ounce) cans whole kernel corn, drained	3 (438 g)
1 red bell pepper, chopped	1
1 cup chopped walnuts	250 ml
¾ cup chopped celery	180 ml
1 (8 ounce) bottle Italian salad dressing	1 (228 g)

1. In bowl with lid, combine corn, bell pepper, walnuts and celery. (For a special little zip, add several dashes of hot sauce.)
2. Pour salad dressing over vegetables.
3. Refrigerate several hours before serving.

Mediterranean Potato Salad

2 pounds new red-skinned potatoes, quartered	**1 kg**
¾ to 1 cup Caesar dressing	**180 to 250 ml**
½ cup grated parmesan cheese	**125 ml**
¼ cup chopped fresh parsley	**60 ml**
½ cup chopped roasted red peppers	**125 ml**

1. Cook potatoes in boiling water until fork-tender and drain
2. Pour dressing over potatoes in large bowl.
3. Add cheese, parsley and peppers and toss lightly. Serve warm or chilled.

Pineapple Slaw

1 (8 ounce) can unsweetened pineapple tidbits with juice	**1 (228 g)**
3 cups finely shredded cabbage	**750 ml**
1½ cups, chopped red delicious apple with peel	**375 ml**
½ cup chopped celery	**125 ml**
¾ cup mayonnaise	**180 ml**

1. Drain pineapple and reserve 3 tablespoons (45 ml) juice. Combine pineapple, cabbage, apple and celery in large bowl. (Add dressing quickly after cutting apple so apple will not darken.)
2. Combine reserved juice and mayonnaise, add to cabbage mixture and toss gently. Cover, and chill.

Calypso Coleslaw

1 (16 ounce) package shredded cabbage	1 (454 g)
1 bunch green onions with tops, sliced	1
2 cups cubed cheddar cheese or mozzarella cheese	500 ml
¼ cup sliced ripe olives	60 ml
1 (15 ounce) can whole kernel corn with peppers, drained	1 (438 g)

1. Combine all slaw ingredients and a few sprinkles of salt.

Dressing for Calypso Coleslaw

1 cup mayonnaise	250 ml
2 tablespoons sugar	30 ml
1 tablespoon prepared mustard	15 ml
2 tablespoons vinegar	30 ml

1. Combine dressing ingredients and mix well.
2. Add dressing to slaw, toss, cover and refrigerate.

Home-Style Slaw

1 medium green cabbage, shredded	1
½ onion, chopped	½
⅓ cup sugar	80 ml
1 cup mayonnaise	250 ml
¼ cup vinegar	60 ml

1. Toss cabbage and onion seasoned with salt, pepper and sugar.
2. Combine mayonnaise and vinegar. Pour over cabbage and onion, toss and chill.

Easy Guacamole Salad

4 avocados, softened	4
1 (8 ounce) package cream cheese, softened	1 (228 g)
1 (10 ounce) can diced tomatoes and green chilies	1 (284 g)
1½ teaspoons garlic salt	7 ml
About 1 tablespoon lemon juice	15 ml

1. Peel avocados and mash with fork. In mixing bowl, beat cream cheese until smooth, add avocados and remaining ingredients and mix well.
2. This may be served on a lettuce leaf with a few tortilla chips.

Terrific Tortellini Salad

2 (14 ounce) packages frozen cheese tortellini	2 (420 g)
1 green and 1 red bell pepper, diced	1
1 cucumber, chopped	1
1 (14 ounce) can artichoke hearts, rinsed, drain	1 (420 g)
1 (8 ounce) bottle creamy Caesar salad dressing	1 (228 g)

1. Prepare tortellini according to package directions and drain. Rinse with cold water, drain and chill.
2. Combine tortellini and remaining ingredients in large bowl, cover and refrigerate at least 2 hours.

Special Rice Salad

1 (6 ounce) package chicken Rice-a-Roni	**1 (170 g)**
¾ cup chopped green pepper	**180 ml**
1 bunch fresh green onion with tops, chopped	**1**
2 (6 ounce) jars marinated artichoke hearts,	
drained, chopped	**2 (170 g)**
½ to ⅔ cup mayonnaise	**125 to**
	180 ml

1. Cook rice according to directions, but without butter. Drain and cool.
2. Add remaining ingredients, toss and chill.

This rice salad has lots of flavor!

Marinated Cucumbers

3 cucumbers, thinly sliced	**3**
2 (4 ounce) jars chopped pimentos, drained	**2 (115 g)**
⅔ cup oil	**180 ml**
¼ cup white wine vinegar	**60 ml**
1 (8 ounce) carton sour cream	**1 (228 g)**

1. Mix cucumbers and pimentos. Combine oil, vinegar and ½ teaspoon (2 ml) salt. Pour over cucumbers and chill 1 hour.
2. To serve, drain well and pour sour cream over cucumbers and pimentos and toss.

Marinated Brussels Sprouts

2 (10 ounce) boxes frozen brussels sprouts	2 (284 g)
1 cup Italian dressing	250 ml
1 cup chopped green bell pepper	250 ml
½ cup chopped onion	125 ml

1. Pierce box of brussels sprouts and cook in microwave for 7 minutes.
2. Mix Italian dressing, bell pepper and onion.
3. Pour over brussels sprouts and marinate for at least 24 hours. Drain to serve.

Red Hot Onions

3 large purple onions	3
2 tablespoons hot sauce	30 ml
3 tablespoons olive oil	30 ml
3 tablespoons red wine vinegar	30 ml

1. Slice onions thinly. Pour 1 cup (250 ml) boiling water over onions, let stand 1 minute and drain.
2. Mix hot sauce, oil and vinegar and pour over onion rings in shallow bowl. Refrigerate and let stand at least 3 hours. Drain to serve. Good with barbecue.

Fancy Eggs

12 large hard-boiled eggs	12
1 (4 ounce) package crumbled blue cheese	1 (115 g)
¼ cup half-and-half cream	60 ml
2 tablespoons lime juice	30 ml
2 tablespoons black caviar	30 ml

1. Cut eggs in half lengthwise, carefully remove yolks and mash with fork.
2. Add cheese, half-and-half and lime juice and stir until smooth. Spoon back into egg whites.
3. Top with caviar and refrigerate.

Chicken Salad

3 cups finely chopped, cooked chicken breasts	750 ml
1½ cups chopped celery	375 ml
½ cup sweet pickle relish	125 ml
2 hard-boiled eggs, chopped	2
¾ cup mayonnaise	180 ml

1. Combine all ingredients and several sprinkles salt and pepper.

*Adding ½ cup (125 ml) chopped pecans gives
the chicken salad a special taste.*

Creamy Orange Salad

1 (6 ounce) package orange gelatin	1 (170 g)
1 (8 ounce) package cream cheese, softened	1 (228 g)
1 (14 ounce) can sweetened condensed milk	1 (420 g)
1 (8 ounce) carton whipped topping	1 (228 g)
2 (11 ounce) cans mandarin orange slices, drained	2 (312 g)

1. In bowl, dissolve gelatin in 1¼ cups (310 ml) boiling water. In mixing bowl, beat cream cheese until fluffy. Gradually blend in hot gelatin and beat on low speed until smooth.
2. Stir in condensed milk and refrigerate until mixture begins to thicken. Fold in whipped topping and orange slices.
3. Spoon into 9 x 13-inch (23 x 33 cm) glass dish. Refrigerate 4 hours before serving.

Fantastic Fruit Salad

2 (11 ounce) cans mandarin oranges	2 (312 g)
2 (15 ounce) cans pineapple chunks	2 (438 g)
1 (16 ounce) carton frozen strawberries, thawed	1 (454 g)
1 (20 ounce) can peach pie filling	1 (570 g)
1 (20 ounce) can apricot pie filling	1 (570 g)

1. Drain oranges, pineapple and strawberries. Combine all ingredients and fold together gently.
2. If you like, add 2 sliced bananas to salad.

Peachy Fruit Salad

2 (20 ounce) cans peach pie filling	2 (570 g)
1 (20 ounce) can pineapple chunks, drained	2 (570 g)
1 (11 ounce) can mandarin oranges, drained	2 ((312 g)
1 (8 ounce) jar maraschino cherries, drained	1 (228 g)
1 cup miniature marshmallows	250 ml

1. Combine all ingredients in large bowl, fold together gently and refrigerate.
2. Serve in pretty crystal bowl. (Bananas may be added if you like.)

Fluffy Fruit Salad

2 (20 ounce) cans pineapple tidbits, drained	2 (570 g)
1 (16 ounce) can whole cranberry sauce	1 (454 g)
2 (11 ounce) cans mandarin oranges, drained	1 (312 g)
½ cup chopped pecans	125 ml
1 (8 ounce) carton whipped topping	1 (228 g)

1. In bowl, combine pineapple, cranberries, oranges and pecans.
2. Fold in whipped topping.
3. Serve in pretty crystal bowl.

Cherry Salad

1 (20 ounce) can cherry pie filling	1 (570 g)
1 (20 ounce) can crushed pineapple, drained	1 (570 g)
1 (14 ounce) can sweetened condensed milk	1 (420 g)
1 cup miniature marshmallows	250 ml
1 cup chopped pecans	250 ml
1 (8 ounce) carton whipped topping	1 (228 g)

1. In large bowl, combine pie filling, pineapple, condensed milk, marshmallows and pecans.
2. Fold in whipped topping, chill and serve in pretty crystal bowl.
3. You may add a couple drops of red food coloring if you like a brighter color.

Cottage Cheese and Fruit Salad

1 (16 ounce) carton small curd cottage cheese	1 (454 g)
1 (6 ounce) package orange gelatin	1 (170 g)
2 (11 ounce) cans mandarin oranges, drained	2 (312 g)
1 (20 ounce) can chunk pineapple, drained	1 (570 g)
1 (8 ounce) carton whipped topping	1 (228 g)

1. Sprinkle gelatin over cottage cheese and mix well. Add oranges and pineapple and mix well.
2. Fold in whipped topping and chill. Pour into pretty crystal bowl.

Angel Salad

1 (8 ounce) package cream cheese, softened	1 (228 g)
½ cup sugar	125 ml
1 (16 ounce) can chunky fruit cocktail, drained	1 (454 g)
1 (15 ounce) can pineapple chunks, drained	1 (438 g)
1 (8 ounce) carton whipped topping	1 (228 g)

1. With mixer, beat cream cheese and sugar until creamy. Add fruit and mix gently.
2. Fold in whipped topping. Pour into crystal bowl and refrigerate.

Strawberry-Rhubarb Salad

2 cups diced frozen rhubarb	500 ml
¾ cup sugar	180 ml
¼ cup water	60 ml
1 (3 ounce) package strawberry gelatin	1 (85 g)
1½ cups whipped topping	375 ml

1. In saucepan, bring rhubarb, sugar and water to boil. Reduce heat, simmer, uncovered for 3 to 5 minutes or until rhubarb softens.
2. Remove from heat and stir in gelatin until it dissolves. Pour into bowl and refrigerate for 30 minutes or until partially set.
3. Fold in whipped topping. Pour into serving dish and chill until firm.

Peaches 'N Cream Salad

1 (6 ounce) package lemon gelatin	1 (170 g)
1 cup boiling water	250 ml
1 (8 ounce) package cream cheese, softened	1 (228 g)
1 (8 ounce) carton whipped topping	1 (228 g)
1 (20 ounce) can peach pie filling,	1 (570 g)
1 (15 ounce) can sliced peaches, drained	1 (438 g)

1. In mixing bowl, combine gelatin and boiling water. Mix well, pour half into separate bowl and set aside.
2. With gelatin in mixing bowl, add cream cheese and beat very slowly until smooth and creamy. Place in refrigerator just until it begins to thicken but not set. Fold in whipped topping and pour into 9 x 13-inch (23 x 33 cm) glass dish. Refrigerate until set.
3. With remaining gelatin, mix in peach pie filling and sliced peaches. Pour over first layer and refrigerate several hours.

Butter-Mint Salad

1 (6 ounce) box lime gelatin	1 (170 g)
1 (20 ounce) can crushed pineapple with juice	1 (570 g)
½ (10 ounce) bag miniature marshmallows	½ (284 g)
1 (8 ounce) carton whipped topping	1 (228 g)
1 (8 ounce) bag buttermints, crushed	1 (228 g)

1. Pour dry gelatin over pineapple. Add marshmallows and set overnight at room temperature.
2. Fold in whipped topping and buttermints. Pour into 9 x 13-inch (23 x 33 cm) dish and freeze.

This salad is so good served with the Hawaiian Chicken.

Cream Cheese-Mango Salad

1 (15 ounce) can mangos   1 (438 g)
1 (6 ounce) packages lemon gelatin   1 (170 g)
2 (8 ounces) cream cheese, softened   2 (228 g)

1. Drain juice from mangos. Combine juice and enough water
   to make 1⅓ cups (330 ml) liquid. Bring to boil and add gelatin.
   Stir until it dissolves.
2. In mixing bowl, cream mangos
   and cream cheese.
3. Mix into hot gelatin and pour into
   muffin tins or a mold.

Tropical Mango Salad

2 (15 ounce) cans mangoes with juice   2 (438 g)
1 (6 ounce) package orange gelatin   1 (170 g)
1 (8 ounce) package cream cheese, softened   1 (228 g)
½ (8 ounce) carton whipped topping   ½ (228 g)

1. Place all mango slices on dinner plate and with knife and fork,
   cut slices into bite-size pieces. Place 1½ cups (375 ml) mango
   juice (add water to make 1½ cups (375 ml)) in saucepan and
   bring to boiling point. Pour over gelatin in mixing bowl and
   mix well.
2. Add cream cheese and start mixer very slowly. Gradually
   increase speed until cream cheese mixes into gelatin. Pour in
   mango pieces. Place in refrigerator until it congeals lightly.
3. Fold in whipped topping, pour into 7 x 11-inch (18 x 28 cm)
   dish and chill.

Luscious Strawberry Salad

1 (6 ounce) package strawberry gelatin	1 (170 g)
2 (10 ounce) boxes frozen strawberries, thawed	2 (284 g)
3 bananas, sliced	3
1 (8 ounce) carton sour cream	1 (228 g)

1. Dissolve gelatin in 1¼ cups (310 ml) boiling water and mix well. Add strawberries and bananas. Pour half mixture in 7 x 11-inch (18 x 28 cm) dish and leave bananas in bottom layer. Chill until firm
2. Spread sour cream over firm gelatin. Add remaining gelatin over sour cream and chill until firm.

★

Holiday Cheer

2 cups ginger ale	500 ml
1 (6 ounce) package orange gelatin	1 (170 g)
1 cup wine	250 ml
1 (9 ounce) package condensed mincemeat	1 (240 g)
1 cup chopped pecans	250 ml

1. Heat ginger ale, stir into gelatin and mix well.
2. Add wine, mincemeat and pecans. Pour into 9 x 13-inch (23 x 33 cm) glass dish and chill.

Pistachio Salad (or Dessert)

1 (20 ounce) can crushed pineapple with juice	1 (570 g)
1 (3 ounce) package instant pistachio pudding mix	1 (85 g)
2 cups miniature marshmallows	500 ml
1 cup chopped pecans	250 ml
1 (8 ounce) carton whipped topping	1 (228 g)

1. Place pineapple in large bowl and sprinkle with dry pudding mix.
2. Add marshmallows and pecans and fold in whipped topping. Pour into crystal serving dish and chill.

Serendipity Salad

1 (6 ounce) package raspberry gelatin	1 (170 g)
1 (16 ounce) can fruit cocktail with juice	1 (454 g)
1 (8 ounce) can crushed pineapple with juice	1 (228 g)
2 bananas, cut into small chunks	2
1 cup miniature marshmallows	250 ml

1. Dissolve gelatin in 1 cup (250 ml) boiling water and mix well.
2. Add fruit cocktail and pineapple and chill until gelatin begins to thicken.
3. Add bananas and marshmallows and pour into sherbet dishes. Cover with plastic wrap and refrigerate. You could also pour salad into 7 x 11-inch (18 x 28 cm) glass dish and cut into squares to serve.

Pink Salad

1 (6 ounce) package raspberry gelatin	1 (170 g)
1 (20 ounce) can crushed pineapple with juice	1 (570 g)
1 cup cream-style cottage cheese	250 ml
1 (8 ounce) carton whipped topping	1 (228 g)
¼ cup chopped pecans	60 ml

1. Place gelatin in large bowl. Heat juice from pineapple and enough water to make 1¼ cups (310 ml). Pour over gelatin and mix well.
2. Cool in refrigerator until gelatin just begins to thicken. Fold in cottage cheese, whipped topping and pecans.
3. Pour into molds or 9 x 13-inch (23 x 33 cm) dish and refrigerate.

Divinity Salad

1 (6 ounce) package lemon gelatin	1 (170 g)
1 (8 ounce) package cream cheese, softened	1 (228 g)
¾ cup chopped pecans	180 ml
1 (15 ounce) can crushed pineapple with juice	1 (438 g)
1 (8 ounce) carton whipped topping	1 (228 g)

1. With mixer, blend gelatin with 1 cup (250 ml) boiling water until it dissolves.
2. Add cream cheese, beat slowly and increase until smooth. Add pecans and pineapple and cool in refrigerator until nearly set.
3. Fold in whipped topping. Pour into 9 x 13-inch (23 x 33 cm) dish and refrigerate.

Purple Lady Salad

1 (6 ounce) box grape gelatin	1 (170 g)
1 (20 ounce) can blueberry pie filling	1 (570 g)
1 (20 ounce) can crushed pineapple with juice	1 (570 g)
1 cup miniature marshmallows	250 ml
1 cup chopped pecans	250 ml

1. In large bowl, pour 1 cup (250 ml) boiling water over gelatin and mix well.
2. Add blueberry pie filling and pineapple. Place in refrigerate until gelatin begins to thicken. Stir in marshmallows and pecans. Pour into 9 x 13-inch (23 x 33 cm) glass dish and chill. (To make a completely different salad, you may fold in 8-ounce (228 g) carton whipped topping when mixture begins to congeal.)

Cherry-Cranberry Salad

1 (6 ounce) package cherry gelatin	1 (170 g)
1 cup boiling water	250 ml
1 (20 ounce) can cherry pie filling	1 (570 g)
1 (16 ounce) can whole cranberry sauce	1 (454 g)

1. In mixing bowl, combine cherry gelatin and boiling water and mix until gelatin dissolves.
2. Mix pie filling and cranberry sauce into gelatin.
3. Pour into 9 x 13-inch (23 x 33 cm) dish and refrigerate.

Creamy Cranberry Salad

1 (6 ounce) package cherry gelatin	1 (170 g)
1 (8 ounce) carton sour cream	1 (228 g)
1 (16 ounce) can whole cranberry sauce	1 (454 g)
1 (5 ounce) can crushed pineapple with juice	1 (438 g)

1. Dissolve gelatin in 1¼ cups (310 ml) boiling water and mix well.
2. Stir in remaining ingredients and pour into 7 x 11-inch (18 x 28 cm) glass dish. Refrigerate until firm.

Cashew Salad

1 (6 ounce) package lemon gelatin	1 (170 g)
1 quart vanilla ice cream	1 L
1 (15 ounce) can fruit cocktail, drained	1 (438 g)
1 cup chopped cashew nuts	250 ml

1. Dissolve gelatin in 1 cup (250 ml) boiling water and stir in ice cream. Blend until ice cream melts.
2. Add fruit cocktail and cashew nuts and mix well.
3. Pour into 7 x 11-inch (18 x 28 cm) glass dish and refrigerate overnight.

Cinnamon-Apple Salad

1 cup cinnamon red hot candies	250 ml
1 (6 ounce) package cherry gelatin	1 (170 g)
1 (16 ounce) jar applesauce	1 (454 g)
1 cup chopped pecans	250 ml
Sour cream	

1. Heat cinnamon red hots in 1¼ cups (310 ml) boiling water until candy melts. While mixture is still hot, pour over gelatin and mix well.
2. Add applesauce and chopped pecans and mix well.
3. Pour into 7 x 11-inch (18 x 28 cm) glass dish and refrigerate until firm. When serving, cut in squares and place dollop of sour cream on top of salad.

Frozen Dessert Salad

1 (8 ounce) package cream cheese, softened	1 (228 g)
1 cup powdered sugar	250 ml
1 (10 ounce) box frozen strawberries, thawed	1 (284 g)
1 (15 ounce) can crushed pineapple, drained	1 (438 g)
1 (8 ounce) carton whipped topping	1 (228 g)

1. In mixing bowl, beat cream cheese and sugar.
2. Fold in remaining ingredients. (This will be even better if you stir in ¾ cup (180 ml) chopped pecans.)
3. Pour into 9 x 9-inch (23 x 23 cm) pan and freeze. Cut into squares to serve.

Frozen Cherry Salad

1 (8 ounce) package cream cheese, softened	1 (228 g)
1 (8 ounce) carton whipped topping	1 (228 g)
1 (20 ounce) can cherry pie filling	1 (570 g)
2 (11 ounce) cans mandarin oranges, drained	2 (312 g)
¾ cup coarsely chopped pecans	180 ml

1. With mixer, beat cream cheese until smooth. Fold in whipped topping.
2. Stir in pie filling, oranges and pecans.
3. Transfer to 9 x 5-inch (23 x 13 cm) loaf pan. Cover and freeze overnight. Remove from freezer 15 minutes before slicing. Serve on lettuce leaf.

Frozen Cranberry-Pineapple Salad

1 (20 ounce) can crushed pineapple, drained	1 (570 g)
2 (16 ounce) cans whole cranberry sauce	2 (454 g)
1 (8 ounce) carton sour cream	1 (228 g)
¾ cup chopped pecans	180 ml

1. In large bowl, combine all ingredients.
2. Pour into sprayed 7 x 11-inch (18 x 28 cm) glass dish.
3. Freeze several hours before serving.

Hot Bunwiches

8 hamburger buns	**8**
8 slices Swiss cheese	**8**
8 slices ham	**8**
8 slices turkey	**8**
8 slices American cheese	**8**

1. Lay out all 8 buns. On bottom, place slices of Swiss cheese, ham, turkey and American cheese. Place top bun over American cheese. Wrap each bunwich individually in foil and place in freezer.
2. When ready to serve, take out of freezer 2 to 3 hours before serving.
3. Heat at 325° (163° C) for about 30 minutes. Serve hot.

Grilled Bacon-Banana Sandwiches

Peanut butter	
8 slices English muffins	**8**
2 bananas	**2**
8 slices bacon, crispy cooked	**8**
Butter, softened	

1. Spread peanut butter over 8 slices of muffins. Slice bananas and arrange on top of 4 slices.
2. Place 2 strips bacon on each of 4 slices. Top with remaining muffin slices. Spread top slice with butter.
3. Brown sandwiches, butter side down. Turn, spread butter and cook other side until golden brown. Serve hot.

Reuben Sandwiches

For each sandwich: 2 slices rye bread	2
1 slice Swiss cheese	1
A generous slice corned beef	
2 tablespoons sauerkraut	30 ml
Dijon mustard	

1. Butter 1 slice bread on 1 side. Place butter side down in skillet over low heat.
2. Layer on bread: cheese, corned beef, sauerkraut and spread mustard on 1 side of other slice; butter opposite side. Place butter side up on sauerkraut.
3. Cook until bottom browns, turn carefully and brown other side.

Pizza Sandwich

1 (14 ounce) package English muffins	1 (420 g)
1 pound bulk sausage, cooked, drained	454 g
1½ cups pizza sauce	375 ml
1 (4 ounce) can mushrooms, drained	1 (115 g)
1 (8 ounce) package shredded mozzarella cheese	1 (228 g)

1. Split muffins and layer ingredients on each muffin half, ending with cheese.
2. Broil until cheese melts.

Turkey-Asparagus Sandwiches

4 (1 ounce) slices cheddar cheese	4 (28 g)
2 English muffins, split, toasted	2
½ pound thinly sliced turkey	228 g
1 (15 ounce) can asparagus spears	1 (438 g)
1 package hollandaise sauce mix	1

1. Place cheese slice on each muffin half and top evenly with turkey.
2. Cut asparagus spears to fit muffin halves and top each sandwich with 3 or 4 asparagus spears. Reserve remaining asparagus for another use.
3. Prepare sauce mix according to package directions and pour evenly over sandwiches. Sprinkle with paprika if desired.

Turkey-Cranberry Croissant

1 (8 ounce) package cream cheese, softened	1 (228 g)
¼ cup orange marmalade	60 ml
6 large croissants, split	6
Lettuce leaves	
1 pound thinly sliced cooked turkey	454 g
¾ cup whole berry cranberry sauce	180 ml

1. Beat cream cheese and orange marmalade. Spread evenly on cut sides of croissants.
2. Place lettuce leaves and turkey on croissant bottoms and spread with cranberry sauce.
3. Cover with croissant tops.

Provolone-Pepper Burgers

⅓ cup finely cubed provolone cheese	80 ml
¼ cup diced roasted red peppers	60 ml
¼ cup finely chopped onion	60 ml
1 pound lean ground beef	454 ml
4 hamburger buns, split	4

1. In bowl, combine cheese, red peppers, onion and a little salt and pepper. Add beef and mix well. Shape into 4 patties.
2. Grill covered, over medium-hot heat for 5 minutes on each side or until meat is no longer pink.
3. Add your favorite lettuce, tomatoes, etc.

Meatball Hoagies

1 small onion, diced	1
1 small green bell pepper, diced	1
1 (15 ounce) can sloppy joe sauce	1 (438 g)
30 to 32 frozen cooked meatballs	30 to 32
4 hoagie buns	4

1. Saute onion and pepper in 1 tablespoon (15 ml) oil.
2. Add sauce and meatballs; cook 10 minutes or until thoroughly heated, stirring often.
3. Spoon evenly onto hoagie buns.

Sloppy Joes

1 pound lean ground beef	454 g
1 (10 ounce) can Italian tomato soup	1 (284 g)
2 teaspoons worcestershire	10 ml
⅛ teaspoon black pepper	.5 ml
6 hamburger buns, split, toasted	6

1. In skillet, cook beef until brown and stir to separate meat. Spoon off fat.
2. Add soup, ¼ cup (60 ml) water, worcestershire and pepper. Heat thoroughly and stir often.
3. Serve on buns.

Party Sandwiches

1 (8 ounce) package cream cheese, softened	1 (228 g)
⅓ cup chopped stuffed olives	80 ml
2 tablespoons olive juice	30 ml
⅓ cup chopped pecans	80 ml
6 slices bacon, cooked, crumbled	6

1. Beat cream cheese with mixer until smooth.
2. Add all other ingredients.
3. Spread on party rye bread.

Spinach Sandwiches

1 (10 ounce) package chopped spinach, thawed, well drained	1 (284 g)
1 cup mayonnaise	250 ml
1 (8 ounce) carton sour cream	1 (228 g)
½ cup finely minced onion	125 ml
1 (1 ounce) envelope dry vegetable soup mix	1 (28 g)

1. Make sure spinach is WELL drained. Add remaining ingredients and mix well. (If you like, ¾ cup (180 ml) finely chopped pecans may be added.)
2. Refrigerate 3 to 4 hours before making sandwiches.
3. To make sandwiches, use thin white bread.

Orange-Cheese Spread

2 (8 ounce) packages cream cheese, softened	2 (228 g)
½ cup powdered sugar	125 ml
1 tablespoon grated orange peel	15 ml
2 tablespoons Grand Marnier	30 ml
2 tablespoons frozen orange juice concentrate, undiluted	30 ml

1. Blend all ingredients in a mixing bowl until smooth and refrigerate.
2. Spread on dessert breads to make sandwiches. This spread is great on poppy seed buns.
3. This may also be used as dip for fruit.

Hot and Sweet Mustard

4 ounces dry mustard	**115 g**
1 cup vinegar	**250 ml**
3 eggs	**3**
1 cup sugar	**250 ml**

1. Soak dry mustard in vinegar overnight.
2. Beat eggs and sugar and add to vinegar-mustard mixture. In top of double boiler, cook over low heat for approximately 15 minutes, stirring constantly. Mixture will resemble a custard consistency.
3. Pour immediately into jars. Store in refrigerator. Serve with ham.

Great to keep in the refrigerator for ham sandwiches.

Remoulade Mayonnaise

1 cup mayonnaise	**250 ml**
½ cup chunky salsa	**125 ml**
¼ cup sweet pickle relish	**60 ml**
1 teaspoon dijon mustard	**5 ml**
1 tablespoon horseradish	**15 ml**

1. Combine all ingredients and mix well. This is great spread for beef or ham sandwiches and chill.

SANDWICHES EXTRAORDINAIRE

Here are some new or different combinations for sandwiches you may not have tried before. You'll get some "ooh's" and "aah's" and maybe even a raised eyebrow or two.

Corned Beef Sandwich
Pumpernickel bread
Mayonnaise
Deli sliced corned beef
Slices of Swiss cheese
Lettuce

Pastrami-Slaw Sandwich
Hoagie rolls
Grey Poupon mustard
Slices of pastrami
Slices of mozzarella cheese
Deli cold slaw

Ham-Avocado Sandwich
Rye bread
Slices mozzarella cheese
Deli ham salad
Avocado slices
Lettuce

Crab Salad Sandwich
Whole wheat bread
Slices of American cheese
Deli shrimp or crab salad
Slices of avocados
Lettuce

Sauerkraut Sandwich
Dark rye bread
2 slices corned beef
2 slices Swiss cheese
4 tablespoons sauerkraut
Russian dressing

Ham-Sprouts Sandwich
Pita bread
Ham slices
Mozzarella cheese slices
Slices of sweet pickles
Bean sprouts and mayonnaise

Deli Sandwich
French bread slices
Turkey and deli beef slices
Slices of American cheese
Slices of Monterey Jack cheese
Lettuce with mayonnaise

Egg Salad Sandwich
Kaiser rolls
Spread with softened cream
   cheese
Deli egg salad
Slices of dill pickles
Bean sprouts

Turkey-Havarti Sandwich

Multi-grain bread
Deli turkey breasts
Slices havarti cheese
Fresh spinach
Garlic mayonnaise

Turkey-Brie Sandwich

French rolls
Thin slices brie cheese
Deli turkey breast slices
Chutney spread
Mayonnaise

Sweet-Peppered Sandwich

Slices marble rye bread
Slices deli peppered roast beef
Slices sweet onion,
   separated into rings
Leaf lettuce
Horseradish mayonnaise

Spinach Salad Sandwich

Pumpernickel bread
Deli roast beef
Fresh spinach
Tomato slices
Quick guacamole

Hawaiian Sandwich

Kaiser rolls
Grilled chicken breasts
Canned pineapple slices
Leaf lettuce
Sesame-ginger mayonnaise

Bacon-Bibb Sandwich

Honey nut bread
Crisp cooked bacon slices
Tomato slices
Bibb lettuce
Remoulade mayonnaise

Special Sandwich Spreads

Horseradish Mayonnaise:
½ cup (125 ml) mayonnaise
1 tablespoon (15 ml) chopped
  fresh chives
1 tablespoon (15 ml) prepared
  horseradish
⅛ teaspoon (.5 ml) seasoned salt
Combine ingredients. Refrigerate.

Remoulade Spread:
½ cup (125 ml) mayonnaise
2 tablespoons (30 ml) chunky
  salsa
1 teaspoon (5 ml) chopped fresh
  parsley
1 teaspoon (5 ml) sweet pickle
  relish
1 teaspoon (5 ml) dijon mustard
Combine ingredients. Refrigerate.

Sesame-Ginger Mayonnaise:
⅔ cup (160 ml) mayonnaise
1 tablespoon (15 ml) honey
1 tablespoon (15 ml) toasted
  sesame seeds
2 teaspoons (10 ml) grated fresh
  gingerroot
Combine ingredients. Refrigerate.

Garlic Mayonnaise:
⅔ cup (160 ml) mayonnaise
1 tablespoon (15 ml) chopped
  roasted garlic
1 teaspoon (5 ml) finely chopped
  onion
⅛ teaspoon (.5 ml) salt
Combine ingredients. Refrigerate.

Chutney Spread:
⅓ cup (80 ml) peach preserves
½ cup (125 ml) chopped fresh
  peaches
2 teaspoon (10 ml) finely chopped
  green onion
½ teaspoon (2 ml) balsamic
  vinegar
¼ teaspoon (1 ml) crushed red
  pepper flake
Combine ingredients. Refrigerate.

Quick Guacamole:
1 (1 ounce) 1 (28 g) package dry
  onion soup mix
2 (8 ounce) 2 (228 g) cartons
  avocado dip
2 green onions with tops,
  chopped
½ teaspoon (2 ml) crushed dill
  weed
Combine ingredients. Refrigerate.

BURGERS WITH A FLAIR

Basic Burger:

1¼ pounds ground chuck	**570 g**
1 egg	**1**
2 teaspoons worcestershire sauce	**10 ml**
½ teaspoon salt	**2 ml**
¼ teaspoon black pepper	**1 ml**

1. Mix ground chuck with egg, worcestershire, salt and pepper. Form into 4 or 5 patties about ½-inch (1 cm) thick and about 4 inches in diameter. Cook on grill for about 5 to 6 minutes on each side or in skillet for about 4 to 5 minutes on each side. (Ground beef should never be cooked rare.)
2. Toast 4 buns and spread with mayonnaise or mustard.
3. Add lettuce, tomatoes and slice of onion and serve.

Here are some suggested additions to your basic hamburger for a little change of taste.

Super Double-Cheese Burger

Basic burger plus 2 slices crisp, cooked bacon, American cheese and Swiss cheese slices for each bun.

Super Mexi-Burger

Basic burger plus spread some deli-prepared guacamole and sliced hot peppers.

Super Sunny Burger

Basic burger plus instead of lettuce, spread about 3 tablespoons (45 ml) deli-prepared slaw and a few sunflower seeds.

Super Snack Burger

Basic burger plus add thin slices of apples and some chopped peanuts.

Super Cucumber Burger

Basic burger plus add thin slices of cucumber and sliced olives.

Super Monterey Burger

Basic burger plus instead of American cheese, use Monterey Jack cheese. Instead of mayonnaise or mustard, use prepared guacamole as a spread.

Super Pastrami Burger

Basic burger plus add slices of pastrami and slices of mozzarella cheese.

Super Salami Burger

Basic burger plus add slices of salami and slices of Swiss cheese.

Super Avocado-Bacon Burger

Basic burger plus add slices of avocados, mayonnaise (not mustard) and slices of crisp, cooked bacon.

VEGETABLES
&
SIDE DISHES

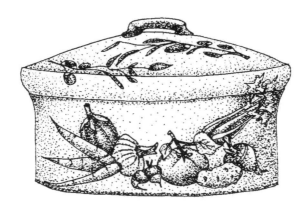

Asparagus Bake

4 (10.5 ounce) cans asparagus	4 (300 g)
3 eggs, hard-boiled, sliced	3
⅓ cup milk	80 ml
1½ cups grated cheddar cheese	375 ml
1¼ cups cheese cracker crumbs	310 ml

1. Place asparagus in 7 x 11-inch (18 x 28 cm) baking dish. Place hard-boiled eggs on top. Pour milk over casserole.
2. Sprinkle cheese on top and add cracker crumbs.
3. Bake uncovered at 350° (176° C) for 30 minutes.

Almond Asparagus

⅓ cup (5 tablespoons) butter	80 ml
1 to 1½ pounds fresh asparagus	454 to 682 g
⅔ cup slivered almonds	160 ml
1 tablespoon lemon juice	15 ml

1. Melt butter in skillet and add asparagus and almonds. Saute 3 to 4 minutes.
2. Cover and steam about 2 minutes or until tender crisp.
3. Sprinkle lemon and a little salt and pepper over asparagus. Serve hot.

Asparagus Caesar

3 (15 ounce) cans asparagus spears, drained	3 (438 g)
¼ cup (½ stick) butter, melted	60 ml
3 tablespoons lemon juice	45 ml
½ cup grated parmesan cheese	125 ml

1. Place asparagus in 2-quart (2 L) baking dish. Drizzle on butter and lemon juice. Sprinkle with cheese and a little paprika if you like.
2. Bake at 400° (204° C) for 15 to 20 minutes.

Fantastic Fried Corn

2 (16 ounce) packages frozen whole kernel corn	2 (454 g)
½ cup (1 stick) butter	125 ml
1 cup whipping cream	250 ml
1 tablespoon sugar	15 ml
1 teaspoon salt	5 ml

1. Place corn in large skillet and turn on medium heat. Add butter, whipping cream, sugar and salt.
2. Stirring constantly, heat until most of whipping cream and butter absorbs into corn.

Yes, I know this corn has too many calories, but it is my grandkid's favorite vegetable and who can turn grandkids down. (Actually, I only fix it a couple of times a year.)

Shoe-Peg Corn

½ cup (1 stick) butter	125 ml
1 (8 ounce) package cream cheese	1 (228 g)
3 (16 ounce) cans shoe-peg corn, drained	3 (454 g)
1 (4 ounce) can chopped green chilies	1 (115 g)
1½ cups crushed cracker crumbs	375 ml

1. Melt butter in saucepan and stir in cream cheese. Mix until cream cheese melts.
2. Add corn and chilies. (Salt and pepper if you like.) Mix and pour into greased baking dish.
3. Sprinkle cracker crumbs over casserole. Bake at 350° (176° C) for 25 minutes.

Super Corn Casserole

1 (15 ounce) can whole kernel corn	1 (438 g)
1 (15 ounce) can cream-style corn	1 (438 g)
½ cup (1 stick) butter, melted	125 ml
1 (8 ounce) carton sour cream	1 (228 g)
1 (6 ounce) package jalapeno cornbread mix	1 (170 g)

1. Mix all ingredients and pour into greased 9 x 13-inch (23 x 33 cm) baking dish.
2. Bake uncovered at 350° (176° C) for 35 minutes.
3. It is really tasty if you add ½ cup (125 ml) grated cheese on top immediately after it comes out of oven.

Vegetable-Corn Medley

1 (10 ounce) can golden corn soup	1 (284 g)
½ cup milk	125 ml
2 cups fresh broccoli flowerets	500 ml
2 cups cauliflower flowerets	500 ml
1 cup shredded cheddar cheese	250 ml

1. In saucepan over medium heat, heat soup and milk to boiling, stirring often. Stir in broccoli and cauliflowerets. Return to boiling.
2. Reduce heat to low and cover. Cook 20 minutes or until vegetables are tender and stir occasionally.
3. Stir in cheese and heat until cheese melts.

Green Chili-Corn Casserole

2 (10 ounce) packages frozen whole kernel corn	2 (284 g)
2 tablespoons butter	30 ml
1 (8 ounce) package cream cheese	1 (228 g)
1 tablespoon sugar	15 ml
1 (4 ounce) can chopped green chilies	1 (115 g)

1. Cook corn according to package directions; drain and set aside.
2. Melt butter in saucepan over low heat and add cream cheese and stir until it melts. Stir in corn, sugar and green chilies. Spoon into greased 2-quart (2 L) baking dish.
3. Cover and bake at 350° (176° C) for 25 minutes.

Corn and Okra Jambalaya

¼ pound bacon	115 g
1 pound fresh okra, sliced	454 g
2 onions, chopped	2
1 (16 ounce) can stewed tomatoes	1 (454 g)
1 (16 ounce) can whole kernel corn, drained	1 (454 g)

1. Fry bacon in large skillet until crisp and drain. In same skillet with bacon drippings, saute okra and onions but do not brown.
2. Add tomatoes and corn and bring to a boil. Simmer about 5 to 10 minutes. Jambalaya must not be runny.
3. Serve over hot rice. Sprinkle bacon over top of each serving.

Almond-Green Beans

⅓ cup slivered almonds	80 ml
¼ cup (½ stick) butter	60 ml
¾ teaspoon garlic salt	4 ml
3 tablespoons lemon juice	45 ml
2 (16 ounce) cans french-style green beans	2 (454 g)

1. In saucepan, cook almonds in butter, garlic salt and lemon juice until slightly golden brown.
2. Add drained green beans to almonds and heat.

Green Bean Revenge

3 (16 ounce) cans green beans, drained	3 (454 g)
1 (8 ounce) can sliced water chestnuts, drained, chopped	1 (228 g)
2 (8 ounce) jars jalapeno processed cheese spread	2 (228 g)
1½ cups cracker crumbs	375 g
¼ cup (½ stick) butter, melted	60 ml

1. Place green beans in greased 9 x 13-inch (23 x 33 cm) baking dish and cover with water chestnuts. Heat both jars (take lid off) cheese in microwave just until they can be poured. Pour processed cheese spread over green beans and water chestnuts.
2. Combine cracker crumbs and butter and sprinkle over casserole.
3. Bake at 350° (176° C) for 30 minutes.

Cheesy Green Beans

¾ cup milk	180 ml
1 (8 ounce) package cream cheese	1 (228 g)
½ teaspoon garlic powder	2 ml
½ cup fresh parmesan cheese	125 ml
2 (16 ounce) cans green beans	2 (454 g)

1. In saucepan, combine milk, cream cheese, garlic and parmesan cheese. Heat until cheeses melt.
2. Heat green beans in pan and drain. Cover with cream cheese mixture and toss to coat evenly. Serve hot.

Pine Nut Green Beans

1 (16 ounce) package frozen green beans	1 (454 g)
¼ cup (½ stick) butter	60 ml
⅓ cup pine nuts	80 ml
¼ teaspoon garlic powder	1 ml
Salt and pepper	

1. Cook beans in water in covered 3-quart (3 L) saucepan for 10 to 15 minutes or until tender-crisp and drain.
2. Melt butter in skillet over medium heat and add pine nuts. Cook, stirring frequently, until golden.
3. Add pine nuts to green beans and add seasonings. Serve hot.

Better Butter Beans

1 cup sliced celery	250 ml
1 onion, chopped	1
¼ cup (½ stick) butter	60 ml
1 (10 ounce) can diced tomatoes and green chilies	1 (284 g)
2 (15 ounce) cans butter beans	2 (438 g)

1. Saute celery and onion in butter for about 3 minutes
2. Add tomatoes and chilies, several sprinkles of salt and about ½ teaspoon (2 ml) sugar.
3. Add butter beans, cover and simmer about 20 minutes. Serve hot.

Butter Beans and Green Onions

1 (10 ounce) package frozen butter beans	**1 (284 g)**
6 bacon slices, cooked, drained, crumbled	**6**
1 bunch fresh green onions, chopped	**1**
½ teaspoon garlic powder	**2 ml**
½ cup chopped fresh parsley	**125 ml**

1. Cook butter beans according to package directions and set aside.
2. Saute green onions in bacon drippings. Stir in butter beans, garlic, parsley and a little salt and pepper. Cook just until thoroughly heated.
3. Pour into serving bowl and sprinkle with bacon.

Pine Nut Broccoli

1 bunch fresh broccoli	**1**
¼ cup (½ stick) butter	**60 ml**
½ cup pine nuts	**125 ml**
⅓ cup golden raisins	**80 ml**
2 tablespoons lemon juice	**30 ml**

1. Steam broccoli until tender crisp. In saucepan, place butter, nuts and raisins and saute about 3 minutes.
2. When ready to serve, add lemon juice to nut mixture and pour over broccoli.

Broccoli Supreme

2 (10 ounce) packages broccoli spears	2 (284 g)
1 (6 ounce) stick garlic-cheese roll	1 (170 g)
1 (10 ounce) can cream of mushroom soup	1 (284 g)
1 (3 ounce) can mushrooms, drained	1 (85 g)
¾ cup herb dressing, crushed	180 ml

1. Boil broccoli for 3 minutes and drain.
2. In saucepan, melt cheese on medium heat in mushroom soup and add mushrooms. Combine with broccoli.
3. Pour into 2-quart (2 L) greased baking dish and top with crushed herb dressing. Bake uncovered at 350° (176° C) for 30 minutes.

For a change of pace, use cream of chicken soup instead of mushroom soup and leave off mushrooms.

Heavenly Broccoli

2 (16 ounce) packages frozen broccoli spears	2 (454 g)
1 (8 ounce) container cream cheese and chives	1 (228 g)
2 (10 ounce) cans cream of shrimp soup	2 (284 g)
2 teaspoons lemon juice	10 ml
¼ cup (½ stick) butter, melted	60 ml

1. Trim a little of stems off broccoli and throw away. Cook broccoli in microwave as directed. Place in 2-quart (2 L) baking dish.
2. In saucepan, combine cream cheese, soup, lemon juice and butter. Heat just enough to mix thoroughly. Pour over broccoli.
3. Heat at 350° (176° C) just until hot and bubbly.

Baked Broccoli

2 (10 ounce) packages frozen broccoli spears	**2 (284 g)**
1 (10 ounce) can cream of chicken soup	**1 (284 g)**
⅔ cup mayonnaise	**160 ml**
¾ cup breadcrumbs	**180 ml**
Paprika	

1. Place broccoli spears in baking dish.
2. In saucepan, combine soup and mayonnaise, heat and pour over broccoli. Sprinkle with breadcrumbs and paprika.
3. Bake at 325° (163° C) for 45 minutes.

Parmesan Broccoli

1 (16 ounce) package frozen broccoli spears	**1 (454 g)**
½ teaspoon garlic powder	**2 ml**
½ cup breadcrumbs	**125 ml**
¼ cup (½ stick) butter, melted	**60 ml**
½ cup parmesan cheese	**125 ml**

1. Cook broccoli as directed on package.
2. Drain and add garlic powder, breadcrumbs, butter and cheese. Add salt if you like and toss.
3. Heat and serve.

Broccoli-Stuffed Tomatoes

4 medium tomatoes	4
1 (10 ounce) package frozen chopped broccoli	1 (284 g)
1 (6 ounce) roll garlic cheese, softened	1 (170 g)
½ teaspoon garlic salt	2 ml

1. Cut tops off tomatoes and scoop out pulp. Cook broccoli according to package instruction and drain well. Combine broccoli, cheese and garlic salt. Heat just until cheese melts.
2. Stuff broccoli mixture into tomatoes and place on baking sheet.
3. Bake at 375° (190° C) for about 10 minutes.

Cheddar-Broccoli Bake

1 (10 ounce) can cheddar cheese soup	1 (284 g)
½ cup milk	125 ml
Dash of pepper	
1 (16 ounce) bag frozen broccoli flowerets, cooked	1 (454 g)
1 (6 ounce) can french-fried onion rings	1 (170 g)

1. In 2-quart (2 L) casserole, mix soup, milk, pepper and broccoli.
2. Bake at 350° (176° C) for 25 minutes.
3. Stir and sprinkle onions over broccoli mixture. Bake 5 more minutes or until onions are golden.

Best Cauliflower

1 (16 ounce) package frozen cauliflower	1 (454 g)
Salt and pepper	
1 (8 ounce) carton sour cream	1 (228 g)
1½ cups grated American or cheddar cheese	375 ml
4 teaspoons sesame seeds, toasted	20 ml

1. Cook cauliflower as directed on package. Drain and place half of cauliflower in 2-quart (2 L) baking dish.
2. Sprinkle a little salt and pepper on cauliflower. Spread half of sour cream and half of cheese. Top with 2 teaspoons (10 ml) sesame seeds. Repeat layers.
3. Bake at 350° (176° C) for about 15 to 20 minutes.

Cauliflower Medley

1 head cauliflower, cut into flowerets	1
1 (15 ounce) can Italian stewed tomatoes	1 (438 g)
1 bell pepper, chopped, 1 onion, chopped	1
¼ cup (½ stick) butter	60 ml
1 cup shredded cheddar cheese	250 ml

1. In large saucepan, place cauliflower, stewed tomatoes, bell pepper, onion and butter. Add about 2 tablespoons (30 ml) water and some salt and pepper.
2. Cook, in saucepan with lid on, until cauliflower is done, about 10 to 15 minutes. Do not let cauliflower get mushy.
3. Place in 2-quart (2 L) casserole and sprinkle cheese on top. Bake at 350° (176° C) just until cheese melts.

Seasoned Squash and Onion

8 yellow squash, sliced	8
2 onions, chopped	2
¼ cup (½ stick) butter	60 ml
1 cup grated American cheese	250 ml

1. Cook squash and onion in small amount of water until tender and drain.
2. Add butter and cheese, toss and serve hot.

Chile-Cheese Squash

1 pound yellow squash	454 g
⅔ cup mayonnaise	160 ml
1 (4 ounce) can diced green chilies, drained	1 (115 g)
⅔ cup grated longhorn cheese	160 ml
⅔ cup breadcrumbs	160 ml

1. Cook squash in salted water just until tender-crisp and drain.
2. Return to saucepan, stir in mayonnaise, chilies, cheese and breadcrumbs.
3. Serve hot.

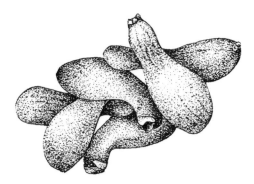

Sunny Yellow Squash

6 to 8 medium yellow squash	6 to 8
1 (8 ounce) package cream cheese, softened	1 (228 g)
2 tablespoons butter	30 ml
1 teaspoon sugar	5 ml

1. In saucepan, cut up squash, add a little water and boil until tender. Drain.
2. Add cream cheese cut in chunks, butter, sugar and a little salt and pepper.
3. Cook over low heat, stirring until cream cheese melts.

Zucchini Patties

1½ cups grated zucchini	375 ml
1 egg, beaten	1
2 tablespoons flour	30 ml
⅓ cup finely minced onion	80 ml
½ teaspoon seasoned salt	2 ml

1. Mix all ingredients.
2. Heat skillet with about 3 tablespoons (45 ml) oil. Drop zucchini mixture by tablespoons onto skillet at medium high heat. Turn and brown both sides.
3. Remove and drain on paper towels.

Creamed Green Peas

1 (16 ounce) package frozen English peas	1 (454 g)
2 tablespoons (¼ stick) butter	30 ml
1 (10 ounce) can cream of celery soup	1 (284 g)
1 (3 ounce) package cream cheese	1 (85 g)
1 (8 ounce) can water chestnuts, drained	1 (228 g)

1. Cook peas in microwave for 8 minutes and turn dish after 4 minutes.
2. In large saucepan, combine butter, soup and cream cheese. Cook on medium heat while stirring, until butter and cream cheese melt.
3. Add peas and water chestnuts and mix. Serve hot.

Country Baked Beans

4 (16 ounce) cans baked beans, drained	4 (454 g)
1 (12 ounce) bottle chili sauce	1 (340 g)
1 large onion, chopped	1
½ pound bacon, cooked, crumbled	228 g
2 cups packed brown sugar	500 ml

1. In ungreased 3-quart (3 L) baking dishes, combine all ingredients and stir until blended.
2. Bake uncovered at 325° (163° C) for 55 minutes or until heated through.

Tasty Black-Eyed Peas

2 (10 ounce) packages frozen black-eyed peas	2 (284 g)
1¼ cups chopped green pepper	310 ml
¾ cup chopped onion	180 ml
3 tablespoons butter	45 ml
1 (15 ounce) can stewed tomatoes with liquid	1 (438 g)

1. Cook black-eyes peas according to package directions and drain.
2. Saute green pepper and onion in butter.
3. Add peas, tomatoes and a little salt and pepper; cook over low heat until thoroughly heated and stir often.

Fried Okra

Fresh small garden okra
Milk or buttermilk
Cornmeal
Salt and pepper

1. Thoroughly wash and drain okra. Cut off top and ends and slice. Toss okra with a little milk or buttermilk (just enough to make cornmeal stick).
2. Sprinkle cornmeal over okra and toss. Heat 2 or 3 tablespoons oil in skillet.
3. Fry okra, turning several times until okra is golden brown and crisp.

Eggplant Fritters

1 medium eggplant	1
1 egg, beaten	1
3 tablespoons flour	45 ml
½ teaspoon salt	2 ml
½ teaspoon baking powder	2 ml

1. Peel and slice eggplant. Steam until tender and drain. Mash until smooth.
2. Add egg, flour, salt and baking powder and mix well.
3. Form into patties and fry in deep hot oil.

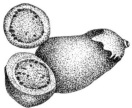

Sauteed Celery

1 bunch celery, chopped diagonally	1
1 (8 ounce) can water chestnuts, drained, chopped	1 (228 g)
¼ cup almonds, toasted	60 ml
¼ cup (½ stick) butter, melted	60 ml

1. Boil celery in salted water just until tender crisp and drain.
2. Saute water chestnuts and almonds in melted butter.
3. Toss celery and water chestnuts-almond mixture. Serve hot.

Tasty Turnips

5 medium turnips	5
2 teaspoons sugar	10 ml
1½ teaspoons salt	7 ml
¼ cup (½ stick) butter, melted	60 ml

1. Peel and dice turnips. Boil with sugar and salt until tender and drain.
2. Add butter to turnips and mash. Serve hot.

Sour Cream Cabbage

1 medium head cabbage, cooked tender crisp, drained	1
2 tablespoons (¼ stick) butter	30 ml
1 tablespoon sugar,	15 ml
¼ teaspoon nutmeg	1 ml
1 (4 ounce) jar pimentos, drained	1 (115 g)
1 (8 ounce) package cream cheese	1 (228 g)

1. Combine cabbage, butter, sugar, nutmeg and pimentos in saucepan.
2. Cook until cabbage is tender-crisp, but don't overcook.
3. Add cream cheese while on low heat. Stir until cream cheese melts.

Spicy Hominy

1 (16 ounce) can yellow hominy, drained	1 (454 g)
1 (8 ounce) carton sour cream	1 (228 g)
1 (4 ounce) can chopped green chiles	1 (115 g)
1¼ cups grated cheddar cheese	310 ml

1. Combine all ingredients and add a little salt.
2. Pour into a 1-quart (1 L) baking dish and bake at 350°
   (176° C) for about 20 minutes.

Creamed Spinach Bake

2 (10 ounce) packages frozen chopped spinach	2 (284 g)
2 (3 ounce) packages cream cheese, softened	2 (85 g)
3 tablespoons butter	45 ml
1 cup seasoned breadcrumbs	250 ml

1. Cook spinach according to package directions and drain.
   Combine cream cheese and butter with spinach. Heat until
   cream cheese and butter melt and mix well with spinach.
   Pour into greased baking dish.
2. Sprinkle a little salt over spinach and cover with breadcrumbs.
3. Bake at 350° (176° C) for 15 to 20 minutes.

Spinach Casserole

1 (16 ounce) package frozen chopped spinach	1 (454 g)
1 (8 ounce) package cream cheese and chives	1 (228 g)
1 (10 ounce) can cream of mushroom soup	1 (284 g)
1 egg, beaten	1
Cracker crumbs	

1. Cook spinach according to directions and drain. Blend cream cheese and soup with egg.
2. Mix with spinach and pour into buttered casserole. Top with cracker crumbs.
3. Bake at 350° (176° C) for 35 minutes.

Cheese-Please Spinach

1 (16 ounce) package frozen chopped spinach	1 (454 g)
3 eggs	3
½ cup flour	125 ml
1 (16 ounce) carton small curd cottage cheese	1 (454 g)
2 cups shredded cheddar cheese	500 ml

1. Cook spinach, drain and set aside. Beat eggs and add flour, cottage cheese and a little salt and pepper. Stir in spinach and cheddar cheese. Pour into 1½-quart (1.5 L) baking dish.
2. Bake uncovered at 350° (176° C) for 35 minutes.

Green Rice and Spinach

1 cup uncooked instant rice	250 ml
1 (10 ounce) package frozen chopped spinach	1 (284 g)
1 onion, finely chopped	1
3 tablespoons butter	45 ml
¾ cup grated cheddar cheese	180 ml

1. Cook rice in large saucepan. Punch holes in box of spinach and cook in microwave about 3 minutes.
2. Reserve 3 tablespoons (45 ml) cheese for topping. Add spinach, onion, butter, cheese, rice and ¼ teaspoon (1 ml) salt. If it seems a little dry, add several tablespoons water. Pour into 2-quart (2 L) greased baking dish.
3. Bake at 350° (176° C) for 25 minutes.

Baked Tomatoes

2 (16 ounce) cans diced tomatoes, drained	2 (454 g)
1½ cups toasted breadcrumbs, divided	375 ml
A scant ¼ cup sugar	60 ml
½ onion, chopped	½
¼ cup (½ stick) butter, melted	60 ml

1. Combine tomatoes, 1 cup (250 ml) breadcrumbs, sugar, onion and butter.
2. Pour into buttered baking dish and cover with remaining breadcrumbs.
3. Bake at 325° (163° C) for 25 to 30 minutes or until crumbs are light brown.

Okra Gumbo

1 large onion, chopped	1
1 pound fresh okra, sliced	454 g
¼ cup (½ stick) butter	60 ml
2 (15 ounce) cans tomatoes	2 (438 g)
1 potato, chopped	1

1. Brown onion and okra in butter.
2. Add tomatoes and potato and bring to boil.
3. Simmer until potatoes are done, about 30 minutes.

Cheesy Vegetable Sauce

½ cup shredded cheddar cheese	125 ml
½ cup sour cream	125 ml
¼ cup (½ stick) butter	60 ml
2 tablespoons chopped fresh parsley	30 ml
½ teaspoon garlic powder	2 ml

1. Combine all ingredients in 3-quart (3 L) glass bowl.
   Microwave at MEDIUM-HIGH for 2 minutes or until cheese
   melts, stirring at 1-minute intervals with wire whisk.
2. Serve over cooked broccoli, cauliflower or even potatoes.

Mixed Vegetable-Cheese Casserole

1 (16 ounce) package frozen mixed vegetables	1 (454 g)
1¾ cups shredded American cheese	430 ml
¾ cup mayonnaise	180 ml
1 tube round buttery crackers, crushed	1
6 tablespoons (¾ stick) butter, melted	90 ml

1. Cook vegetables according to directions and drain. Place in 2-quart (2 L) buttered casserole dish.
2. Mix cheese and mayonnaise and spread over vegetables. Mix cracker crumbs and butter and sprinkle on top.
3. Bake at 350° (176° C) for 35 minutes.

These vegetables are worthy of Sunday dinner and besides that, this is the way to get kids to eat vegetables.

Herb-Seasoned Vegetables

1 (14 ounce) can seasoned chicken broth with Italian herbs	1 (420 g)
½ teaspoon garlic powder	2 ml
1 (16 ounce) package frozen vegetables	1 (454 g)
¼ cup grated parmesan cheese	60 ml

1. Heat broth, garlic and vegetables and heat to a boil.
2. Cover and cook over low heat for 5 minutes or until tender-crisp. Drain.
3. Place in serving dish and sprinkle cheese over vegetables.

Creamy Vegetable Casserole

1 (16 ounce) package frozen broccoli, carrots and cauliflower	1 (454 g)
1 (10 ounce) can cream of mushroom soup	1 (284 g)
1 (8 ounce) carton spreadable garden vegetable cream cheese	1 (228 g)
1 cup seasoned croutons	250 ml

1. Cook vegetables according to package directions; drain and place in a large bowl.
2. Place soup and cream cheese in saucepan and heat just enough to mix easily. Pour into vegetable mixture and mix well. Pour into 2-quart (2 L) baking dish. Sprinkle with croutons.
3. Bake uncovered at 375° (190° C) for 25 minutes or until bubbly.

Baked Beans

2 (15 ounce) cans pork and beans, slightly drained	2 (438 g)
½ onion, finely chopped	½
⅔ cup packed brown sugar,	160 ml
¼ cup chili sauce	60 ml
1 tablespoon worcestershire	15 ml
2 strips bacon	2

1. In bowl, combine beans, onion, brown sugar, chili sauce and worcestershire.
2. Pour into buttered 2-quart (2 L) casserole dish and place bacon strips over beans.
3. Bake uncovered at 325° (163° C) for 50 minutes.

Zucchini au Gratin

6 medium zucchini, sliced	6
1 onion, chopped	1
1 (8 ounce) carton sour cream	1 (228 g)
1¼ cups grated cheddar cheese	310 ml
2 teaspoons sesame seeds, toasted	10 ml

1. Cook zucchini and onion in a little salted water. Do not over cook and drain well.
2. Place half zucchini mixture in buttered 2-quart (2 L) casserole and sprinkle with salt and pepper. Spread with half sour cream and half cheese. Repeat layer.
3. Top with sesame seeds. Bake uncovered at 350° (176° C) about 15 minutes.

Zucchini Bake

4 cups grated zucchini	1 L
1½ cups grated Monterey Jack cheese	375 ml
4 eggs, beaten	4
2 cups cheese crackers crumbs	500 ml

1. In bowl, combine zucchini, cheese and eggs and mix well.
2. Spoon into buttered 3-quart (3 L) baking dish. Sprinkle cracker crumbs over top.
3. Bake uncovered at 350° (176° C) for 35 minutes.

Mashed Potatoes Supreme

1 (8 ounce) package cream cheese, softened	1 (228 g)
½ cup sour cream	125 ml
2 tablespoons (¼ stick) butter, softened	30 ml
1 (1 ounce) envelope ranch salad dressing mix	1 (28 g)
6 to 8 cups warm mashed potatoes (use	
instant)	1.5 to 2 L

1. With mixer, combine cream cheese, sour cream, butter and salad dressing and mix well. Add potatoes and stir well.
2. Transfer to a 1-quart (1 L) casserole dish.
3. Bake at 350° (176° C) for 25 minutes or until heated through.

Creamy Mashed Potatoes

6 large potatoes	6
1 (8 ounce) carton sour cream	1 (228 g)
1 (8 ounce) package cream cheese, softened	1 (228 g)
1 teaspoon salt	5 ml
½ teaspoon white pepper	2 ml

1. Peel, cut up and boil potatoes. Drain. Add sour cream, cream cheese, salt and pepper. Whip until cream cheese melts. Pour into greased 3-quart (3 L) baking dish.
2. Cover with foil and bake at 325° (163° C) for about 20 minutes. (About 10 minutes longer if reheating.)

Ranch Mashed Potatoes

4 cups prepared, unsalted mashed potatoes (use instant)	1 L
1 (1 ounce) envelope ranch-style dressing mix	1 (28 g)
¼ cup (½ stick) butter	60 ml

1. Combine all ingredients in saucepan. Heat on low until potatoes are thoroughly heated.

Loaded Baked Potatoes

6 medium to large potatoes	6
1 (1 pound) hot sausage	1 (454 g)
2 (16 ounce) packages cubed processed cheese	2 (454 g)
1 (10 ounce) can tomatoes and green chilies	1 (284 g)

1. Wrap potatoes in foil and bake at 375° (190° C) for 1 hour or until done.
2. Brown sausage and drain. Add cheese to sausage. Heat until cheese melts and add tomatoes and green chilies.
3. Serve sausage-cheese mixture over baked potatoes.

Broccoli-Cheese Potato Topper

1 (10 ounce) can fiesta nacho cheese soup	1 (284 g)
2 tablespoons sour cream	30 ml
½ teaspoon dijon mustard	2 ml
1 (10 ounce) box frozen broccoli flowerets, cooked	1 (284 g)
4 medium potatoes, baked, fluffed	4

1. In 1-quart microwave-safe baking dish, stir soup, sour cream, mustard and broccoli. Heat in microwave 2 to 2½ minutes.
2. Spoon over potato halves.

Scalloped Potatoes

6 medium potatoes	6
½ cup (1 stick) butter	125 ml
1 tablespoon flour	15 ml
2 cups grated cheddar cheese	500 ml
¾ cup milk	180 ml

1. Peel and slice half potatoes and place in 3-quart (3 L) greased baking dish. Slice half butter over potatoes. Sprinkle flour over potatoes. Cover with half cheese.
2. Repeat layers with cheese on top. Pour milk over casserole and sprinkle on a little pepper. (Prepare potatoes as fast as you can so they will not turn dark.)
3. Cover and bake at 350° (176° C) for 1 hour.

Potatoes Au Gratin

1 (8 ounce) package cube processed cheese	1 (228 g)
1 pint half-and-half cream	500 ml
1 cup shredded cheddar cheese	250 ml
½ cup (1 stick) butter	125 ml
1 (2 pound) package frozen hash brown potatoes	1 (1 kg)

1. In double boiler, melt cheese, cream, cheddar cheese and butter. Place hash brown in greased 9 x 13-inch (23 x 33 cm) baking dish. Pour cheese mixture over potatoes.
2. Bake uncovered at 350° (176° C) for 1 hour.

Twice-Baked Potatoes

8 medium baking potatoes	8
2 tablespoons butter	30 ml
½ teaspoon salt	2 ml
1 (10 ounce) can cheddar cheese soup	1 (284 g)
1 tablespoon chopped dried chives	15 ml

1. Bake potatoes until done. Cut potatoes in half lengthwise and scoop out insides leaving thin shell. With mixer, whip potatoes with butter and salt.
2. Gradually add soup and chives and beat until light and fluffy. (If you want a little "zip" to potatoes, add 1 (10 ounce) (284 g) can fiesta nacho cheese soup instead of cheese soup.)
3. Spoon into shells and sprinkle with paprika. Bake at 425° (218° C) for 15 minutes.

Chive-Potato Souffle

3 eggs, separated	3
2 cups hot mashed potatoes (use instant)	500 ml
½ cup sour cream	125 ml
2 heaping tablespoons chopped chives	30 ml
1 teaspoon seasoned salt	5 ml

1. Beat egg whites until stiff and set aside. Beat yolks until smooth and add to potatoes.
2. Fold in beaten egg whites, sour cream, chives and salt. Pour into buttered 2-quart (2 L) baking dish.
3. Bake at 350° (176° C) for 45 minutes.

Cheddar-Potato Strips

3 large potatoes, cut into ½-inch strips	3, 1 cm
½ cup milk	250 ml
2 tablespoons (¼ stick) butter	30 ml
½ cup shredded cheddar cheese	125 ml
1 tablespoon minced fresh parsley	15 ml

1. In greased 9 x 13-inch (23 x 33 cm) baking dish, arrange potatoes in a single layer. Pour milk over potatoes. Dot with butter and sprinkle a little salt and pepper.
2. Cover and bake at 400° (204° C) for 30 minutes or until potatoes are tender.
3. Sprinkle with cheese and parsley. Bake uncovered 5 minutes longer.

Oven Fries

5 medium baking potatoes	5
⅓ cup oil	80 ml
¼ teaspoon black pepper	1 ml
¾ teaspoon seasoned salt	4 ml
Paprika	

1. Scrub potatoes and cut each in 6 lengthwise wedges. Place potatoes in shallow baking dish. Combine oil, pepper and seasoned salt and brush potatoes with mixture.
2. Sprinkle lightly with paprika. Bake at 375° (190° C) for about 50 minutes or until potatoes are tender and light brown.
3. Baste twice with remaining oil mixture while baking.

Terrific Taters

5 to 6 medium potatoes	5 to 6
1 (8 ounce) carton sour cream	1 (228 g)
1 (1 ounce) dry package ranch salad dressing	
mix	1 (28 g)
1½ cups shredded cheddar cheese	375 ml
3 pieces bacon, fried, drained, crumbled	3

1. Peel, slice and boil potatoes and drain. Place potatoes in 2-quart (2 L) baking dish.
2. Combine sour cream, salad dressing mix and a little pepper. Toss until potatoes are coated. Sprinkle cheese on top.
3. Bake at 350° (176° C) for about 20 minutes. Sprinkle bacon on top. Serve hot.

Herbed New Potatoes

1½ pounds new potatoes	680 ml
6 tablespoons (¾ stick) butter, sliced	90 ml
¼ teaspoon thyme	1 ml
½ cup chopped fresh parsley	125 ml
½ teaspoon rosemary	2 ml

1. Scrub potatoes and cut in halves but do not peel. In medium saucepan, boil in lightly salted water. Cook until potatoes are tender, about 20 minutes and drain.
2. Add butter, thyme, parsley and rosemary. Toss gently until butter melts.
3. Serve hot.

Carnival Couscous

1 (5.7 ounce) box herbed chicken couscous	1 (110 g)
¼ cup (½ stick) butter	60 ml
1 red bell pepper, minced	1
1 yellow squash, seeded, minced	1
¾ cup fresh broccoli flowerets, finely chopped	180 ml

1. Cook couscous according to package directions, but leave out butter.
2. With butter in saucepan, saute bell pepper, squash and broccoli and cook about 10 minutes or until vegetables are almost tender.
3. Combine couscous and vegetables. (If you want to do this a little ahead of time, place couscous and vegetable in sprayed baking dish. Heat at 325° (163° C) for about 20 minutes).

This is a delicious and colorful dish – a recipe that
takes the place of rice and a vegetable.

Macaroni, Cheese and Tomatoes

2 cups elbow macaroni, uncooked	500 ml
1 (14 ounce) can stewed tomatoes with liquid	1 (420 g)
1 (8 ounce) package shredded cheddar cheese	1 (228 g)
2 tablespoons sugar	30 ml
1 (6 ounce) package cheese slices	1 (170 g)

1. Cook macaroni according to package directions and drain. In large bowl, combine macaroni, tomatoes, shredded cheese, sugar, ¼ cup (60 ml) water and a little salt and mix well.
2. Pour into 9 x 13-inch (23 x 33 cm) baking dish and place cheese slices on top.
3. Bake at 350° (176° C) for 30 minutes or until bubbly.

Red Rice

1 (16 ounce) package smoked sausage, sliced	1 (454 g)
2 (10 ounce) cans diced tomatoes and green chiles	2 (284 g)
3 cups chicken broth	750 ml
2 teaspoons creole seasoning	10 ml
1½ cups uncooked long-grain rice	375 ml

1. Saute sausage in Dutch oven until brown. Stir in tomatoes and green chiles, broth and seasoning and bring to boil.
2. Stir in rice and cover, reduce heat and simmer 25 minutes.
3. Uncover and cook until liquid absorbs.

Green Chili-Rice

1 cup instant rice, cooked	250 ml
1 (12 ounce) package shredded Monterrey	
Jack cheese	1 (340 g)
1 (7 ounce) can chopped green chilies	1 (198 g)
2 (8 ounce) cartons sour cream	2 (228 g)
½ teaspoon garlic powder	2 ml

1. In large bowl, combine and mix all ingredients and add a little salt if you like.
2. Spoon into greased 9 x 13-inch (23 x 33 cm) baking dish and bake covered at 350° (176° C) for 30 minutes.

Grits Souffle

1½ cups grits	375 ml
1½ teaspoon salt	7 ml
½ cup (1 stick) butter	125 ml
1½ cups shredded cheddar cheese	375 ml
5 eggs, beaten	5

1. Boil grits in 6 cups (1.5 L) salted water and drain. Stir in butter and cheese and stir until cheese melts. Allow to cool until lukewarm.
2. Add eggs and pour into greased 2-quart (2 L) baking dish.
3. Bake covered at 350° (176° C) for 45 minutes.

Favorite Pasta

4 ounces spinach linguine, uncooked	**115 g**
1 cup whipping cream	**250 ml**
1 cup chicken broth	**250 ml**
½ cup freshly grated parmesan cheese	**125 ml**
½ cup frozen English peas	**125 ml**

1. Cook linguine according to package directions, drain and keep warm.
2. Combine whipping cream and chicken broth in saucepan and bring to a boil. Reduce heat and simmer 25 minutes or until it thickens and reduces to 1 cup (250 ml). Remove from heat.
3. Add cheese and peas and stir until cheese melts. Toss with linguine and serve immediately.

Pasta With Basil

2½ cups uncooked, small tube pasta	**625 ml**
1 small onion, chopped	**1**
2 tablespoons oil	**30 ml**
2½ tablespoons dried basil	**37 ml**
1 cup shredded mozzarella cheese	**250 ml**

1. Cook pasta according to package directions. In skillet, saute onion in oil.
2. Stir in basil, 1 teaspoon (5 ml) salt and ¼ teaspoon (1 ml) pepper. Cook and stir 1 minute. Drain pasta leaving about ½ cup (125 ml) so pasta won't be too dry and add to basil mixture.
3. Remove from heat and stir in cheese just until it begins to melt. Serve immediately.

Creamy Seasoned Noodles

1 (8 ounce) package wide egg noodles	1 (228 g)
1 (1 ounce) envelope Italian salad dressing mix	1 (28 g)
½ cup whipping cream	125 ml
¼ cup (½ stick) butter	60 ml
¼ cup grated parmesan cheese	60 ml

1. Cook noodles according to package directions and drain.
2. Cut butter in chunks so it will melt easier. Add remaining ingredients and toss lightly to blend thoroughly.
3. Serve hot.

Sweet Potato Wedges

3 pounds sweet potatoes, peeled, quartered lengthwise	1.5 kg
6 tablespoons (¾ stick) butter, melted	90 ml
6 tablespoons orange juice	90 ml
¾ teaspoon salt	4 ml
¾ teaspoon ground cinnamon	4 ml

1. Arrange sweet potatoes in a greased 9 x 13-inch (23 x 33 cm) baking pan Combine butter, orange juice, salt and cinnamon and drizzle over sweet potatoes.
2. Cover and bake at 350° (176° C) for 60 minutes or until tender.

Speedy Sweet Potatoes

2 (16 ounce) cans sweet potatoes, drained	2 (454 g)
1 (8 ounce) can crushed pineapple with juice	1 (228 g)
½ cup chopped pecans	125 ml
⅓ cup packed brown sugar	80 ml
1 cup miniature marshmallows	250 ml

1. In 2-quart (2 L) microwave-safe dish, layer sweet potatoes, a little salt, pineapple, pecans, brown sugar and ½ cup (125 ml) marshmallows. Cover and microwave on high for 6 minutes or until bubbly around edges.
2. Top with remaining marshmallows. Heat uncovered on high for 30 seconds or until marshmallows puff. If you like, sprinkle sweet potatoes with a little nutmeg.

Festive Cranberry Stuffing

1 (14 ounce) can chicken broth	1 (420 g)
1 rib celery, chopped	1
½ cup fresh or frozen cranberries	125 ml
1 small onion, chopped	1
4 cups herb seasoned stuffing	1 L

1. Mix broth, a dash of black pepper, celery, cranberries and onion in saucepan. Heat to a boil. Cover and cook over low heat 5 minutes.
2. Add stuffing and mix lightly. Spoon into baking dish.
3. Heat at 325° (163° C) just until thoroughly heated.

Hopping John

2 (15 ounce) cans jalapeno black-eyed peas with liquid	2 (438 g)
¾ pound ham, chopped	340 g
1 cup chopped onion	250 ml
2 cups hot cooked rice	500 ml
½ cup chopped green onions	125 ml

1. In saucepan, combine peas, ham and onion. Bring to a boil, reduce heat and simmer 15 minutes.
2. Stir in hot rice and green onions. Serve hot.

Maple-Ginger Sweet Potatoes

4 medium sweet potatoes	4
½ cup sour cream	125 ml
⅓ cup maple syrup	80 ml
¼ teaspoon ground ginger	1 ml
¼ cup chopped pecans	60 ml

1. Pierce sweet potatoes several times with fork and place on baking sheet. Bake at 375° (190° C) for 1 hour.
2. Stir sour cream, syrup and ginger. Spoon over split potatoes and sprinkle with pecans.

Whipped Sweet Potatoes

1 (28 ounce) can sweet potatoes, drain most of liquid	1 (800 g)
1 cup (2 sticks) butter, melted, divided	250 ml
1 cup packed light brown sugar	250 ml
1½ cups crushed corn flakes	375 ml

1. Place sweet potatoes in mixing bowl; cut large pieces of potatoes in several pieces. Beat sweet potatoes until creamy. Fold in ¾ cup (1½ sticks) (180 ml) melted butter (do not use margarine) and brown sugar and beat until butter and sugar thoroughly combine with sweet potatoes.
2. Pour into buttered 2-quart (2 L) baking dish. Combine crushed corn flakes and remaining 2 tablespoons (¼ stick) (30 ml) melted butter and sprinkle over sweet potato casserole. (If you like, add ⅓ cup (80 ml) chopped pecans to corn flakes.)
3. Bake uncovered at 350° (176° C) for 40 minutes.

Baked Sweet Potato Topping

4 sweet potatoes	4
6 tablespoons (¾ stick) butter, melted	90 ml
½ cup granulated sugar	125 ml
½ cup packed brown sugar	125 ml
1 teaspoon cinnamon,	5 ml
½ cup flaked coconut	125 ml

1. Prick 4 sweet potatoes several times with fork. Wrap each sweet potato in foil and bake at 375° (190° C) for about 1 hour. Check for doneness. Unwrap sweet potatoes and make slit down center of each potato. Use a fork and fluff up potato.
2. In small bowl, combine melted butter, both sugars, cinnamon and coconut and mix well. Spoon one-fourth of mixture over each potato and again, fluff with fork to make sure sugar mixture goes into each potato.

MAIN DISHES

Chicken Olé

6 boneless, skinless chicken breasts, halved	6
1 (8 ounce) package cream cheese, softened	1 (228 g)
1 (16 ounce) jar salsa	1 (454 g)
2 teaspoons cumin	10 ml
1 cup fresh green onions with tops, chopped	250 ml

1. Pound chicken breasts to flatten. In mixing bowl beat cream cheese until smooth and add salsa, cumin and onions. Place a heaping spoonful of mixture on each chicken breast and roll. Place seam side down, in shallow baking pan.
2. Pour remaining sauce over top of chicken rolls.
3. Bake uncovered at 350° (176° C) for 50 minutes.

~Great Served With~
Easy Guacamole Salad-110 • Shoe-Peg Corn-142

Chicken Crunch

4 boneless, skinless chicken breast halves	4
½ cup Italian salad dressing	125 ml
½ cup sour cream	125 ml
2½ cups crushed corn flakes	625 ml

1. Place chicken in zip-top plastic bag and add salad dressing and sour cream. Seal and refrigerate 1 hour. Remove chicken from marinade and discard marinade.
2. Dredge chicken in corn flakes and place in 9 x 13-inch (23 x 33 cm) baking dish.
3. Bake at 375° (190° C) for 45 minutes.

~Great Served With~
Baked Broccoli-149 • Mediterranean Potato Salad-108

Favorite Chicken Breasts

6 to 8 boneless, skinless chicken breast halves	6 to 8
1 (10 ounce) can cream of mushroom soup	1 (284 g)
¾ cup white wine or white cooking wine	180 ml
1 (8 ounce) carton sour cream	1 (228 g)

1. Place chicken breasts in large, shallow baking pan. Sprinkle on a little salt and pepper. Bake uncovered at 350° (176° C) for 30 minutes.
2. In saucepan, combine soup, wine and sour cream; heat just enough to mix. Remove chicken from oven and pour sour cream mixture over chicken.
3. Return to oven to cook another 30 minutes. Baste twice again. Serve over rice.

~Great Served With~
Broccoli-Cauliflower Salad-100 • Green Chili-Corn Casserole-143

Broccoli-Cheese Chicken

1 tablespoon butter	15 ml
4 boneless, skinless chicken breast halves	4
1 (10 ounce) can condensed broccoli-cheese soup	1 (284 g)
1 (10 ounce) package frozen broccoli spears	1 (284 g)
⅓ cup milk	80 ml

1. In skillet, heat butter and cook chicken 15 minutes or until brown on both sides. Remove and set aside.
2. In same skillet, combine soup, broccoli, milk and a little black pepper. Heat to boiling. Return chicken to skillet. Reduce heat to low.
3. Cover and cook another 25 minutes until chicken is no longer pink and broccoli is tender. Serve over rice.

~Great Served With~
Pine Nut Green Beans-146 • Marinated Cucumbers-111

Hawaiian Chicken

2 small chickens, quartered	**2**
Flour to coat chicken	
Oil	
1 (20 ounce) can sliced pineapple with juice	**1 (570 g)**
2 bell peppers, cut in strips	**2**

1. Pat chicken dry with paper towels. Coat chicken with salt, pepper and flour. Brown chicken in oil and place in shallow pan.
2. Drain pineapple and pour syrup into 2-cup (500 ml) measure. Add water (or orange juice if you have it) to make 1½ cups (375 ml) liquid. Reserve juice for sauce.

Sauce for Hawaiian Chicken:

1 cup sugar	**250 ml**
3 tablespoons cornstarch	**45 ml**
¾ cup vinegar,	**180 ml**
1 tablespoon lemon juice	**15 ml**
1 tablespoon soy sauce	**15 ml**
2 teaspoons chicken bouillon	**10 ml**

1. In medium saucepan, combine 1½ cups (375 ml) juice, sugar, cornstarch, vinegar, lemon juice, soy sauce and chicken bouillon. Bring to a boil, stirring constantly, until it thickens and is clear. Pour over chicken. Bake at 350° (176° C), covered for 40 minutes.
2. Place pineapple slices and bell pepper on top of chicken and bake another 10 minutes. Serve on fluffy white rice.

~Great Served With~
Butter-Mint Salad-118 • Asparagus Bake-140

Apricot Chicken

1 cup apricot preserves	250 ml
1 (8 ounce) bottle Catalina dressing	1 (228 g)
1 (1 ounce) package onion soup mix	1 (28 g)
6 to 8 boneless, skinless	
chicken breast halves	6 to 8

1. In bowl, mix apricot preserves, dressing and soup mix. Place chicken breasts in large, buttered baking dish and pour apricot mixture over chicken. (For a change of pace, use Russian dressing instead of Catalina).
2. Bake uncovered at 325° (163° C) for 1 hour 20 minutes. Serve over hot rice.

~Great Served With~
Asparagus Bake-140 • Nutty Green Salad-105

Pineapple-Teriyaki Chicken

6 boneless, skinless chicken breast halves	6
½ red onion, sliced	½
1 green bell pepper, seeded, sliced	1
1 cup teriyaki marinade with pineapple juice,	
divided	250 ml
1 (15 ounce) can pineapple rings, drained	1 (438 g)

1. Spray 9 x 13-inch (23 x 33 cm) baking dish and place chicken in dish. Arrange vegetables over chicken.
2. Pour marinade over vegetables and chicken.
3. Bake uncovered at 350° (176° C) for 45 minutes. Spoon juices over chicken once during baking. About 10 minutes before chicken is done, place pineapple slices over chicken and return to oven.

~Great Served With~
Broccoli-Waldorf Salad-99 • Asparagus Caesar-141

Hurry-Up Chicken Enchiladas

2½ to 3 cups cooked, cubed chicken breasts	625 to 750 ml
1 (10 ounce) can cream of chicken soup	1 (284 g)
1½ cups chunky salsa, divided	375 ml
8 (6 inch) flour tortillas	8 (15 cm)
1 (10 ounce) can fiesta nacho cheese soup	1 (284 g)

1. In saucepan, combine chicken, soup and ½ cup (125 ml) salsa and heat.
2. Spoon about ⅓ cup (80 ml) chicken mixture down center of each tortilla. Roll up tortilla around filling and place, seam-side down, in sprayed 9 x 13-inch (23 x 33 cm) baking dish.
3. Mix nacho cheese, remaining salsa and ¼ cup (60 ml) water and pour over enchiladas. Cover with wax paper and microwave on high, turning several times, for 5 minutes or until bubbly.

~*Great Served With~*
Green Bean Revenge-145 • Easy Guacamole Salad-110

Dijon Chicken in a Skillet

¼ cup prepared ranch salad dressing	60 ml
1 tablespoon dijon mustard	15 ml
4 boneless, skinless chicken breast halves	4
2 tablespoons (¼ stick) butter	30 ml
3 tablespoons white wine or chicken broth	45 ml

1. In bowl, combine salad dressing and mustard and set aside. In skillet, cook chicken in butter and simmer for 10 to 15 minutes.
2. Add wine or broth and simmer another 20 minutes.
3. Whisk in mustard mixture, cook and stir until blended and heated through. Serve over instant long grain and wild rice.

~Great Served With~
Super Corn Casserole-142 • Broccoli-Noodle Salad-99

Chicken Marseilles

3 tablespoons butter	45 ml
5 to 6 boneless, skinless chicken breast halves	5 to 6
1 (1 ounce) package vegetable soup and dip mix	1 (28 g)
½ teaspoon dill weed	2 ml
½ cup sour cream	125 ml

1. Melt butter in skillet, brown chicken about 10 to 15 minutes and turn occasionally.
2. Stir 2 cups (500 ml) water into skillet with soup mix and dill and bring to a boil. Reduce heat, cover and simmer, stirring occasionally, for 25 to 30 minutes or until chicken is tender. Serve this delicious chicken over instant brown rice. Have rice cooked when chicken cooks. Remove chicken to heated plate.
3. After removing chicken and heat is still on under skillet, stir in sour cream until creamy. Place rice on individual plates or large platter. Lay chicken breasts over rice and spoon sauce over chicken and rice.

This is a simple, but elegant dinner entree. It is not only pleasing to the eye with the colorful vegetables from the soup mix, it also has a wonderful sauce.

~Great Served With~
Summertime-Mushroom Salad-101 • Nutty Green Salad-105

Baked Chicken Poupon

2 tablespoons dijon mustard	30 ml
2 tablespoons oil	30 ml
1 teaspoon garlic powder	5 ml
½ teaspoon Italian seasoning	2 ml
4 boneless, skinless chicken breast halves	4

1. Mix dijon mustard, oil, garlic powder and seasoning in plastic bag. Add chicken breasts and set for 15 minutes.
2. Place chicken in non-stick vegetable sprayed shallow baking pan.
3. Bake uncovered at 375° (190° C) for 35 minutes.

~Great Served With~
Broccoli-Cheese Potato Topper-167
Cottage Cheese and Fruit Salad-116

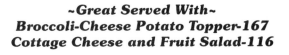

Grilled Chicken Cordon Bleu

6 boneless, skinless chicken breast halves	6
6 slices Swiss cheese	6
6 thin slices deli ham	6
3 tablespoons oil	45 ml
1 cup seasoned breadcrumbs	250 ml

1. Flatten chicken to ¼ inch (.5 cm) thickness. Place 1 slice of cheese and ham on each piece of chicken to within ¼ inch (.5 cm) of edges. Fold in half and secure with toothpicks. Brush with oil and roll in breadcrumbs.
2. Grill, covered, over medium–hot heat for 15 to 18 minutes or until juices run clear.

~Great Served With~
Mediterranean Potato Salad-108
Marinated Brussels Sprouts-112

Chicken Cutlets

6 boneless, skinless chicken breast halves	**6**
1½ cups dry breadcrumbs	**375 ml**
½ cup grated parmesan cheese	**125 ml**
1 teaspoon dried basil	**5 ml**
½ teaspoon garlic powder	**2 ml**
1 (8 ounce) carton sour cream	**1 (228 g)**

1. Flatten chicken to ½-inch (.5 cm) thickness. In shallow dish, combine breadcrumbs, parmesan cheese, basil and garlic powder.
2. Dip chicken in sour cream and coat with crumb mixture. Place in 10 x 15-inch (25 x 38 cm) (so chicken breasts do not touch) greased baking dish.
3. Bake uncovered at 325° (163° C) for 50 to 60 minutes or until golden brown.

~Great Served With~
Carnival Couscous-171 • Pistachio Salad-121

Asparagus-Cheese Chicken

1 tablespoon butter	15 ml
4 boneless, skinless chicken breast halves	4
1 (10 ounce) can condensed broccoli-cheese soup	1 (284 g)
1 (10 ounce) package frozen asparagus cuts	1 (284 g)
⅓ cup milk	80 ml

1. In skillet, heat butter and cook chicken 10 to 15 minutes or until brown on both sides. Remove chicken and set aside.
2. In same skillet, combine soup, asparagus, and milk. Heat to boiling. Return chicken to skillet and reduce heat to low.
3. Cover and cook another 25 minutes until chicken is no longer pink and asparagus is tender.

~Great Served With~
Cream Cheese-Mango Salad-119 • Shoe-Peg Corn-142

One-Dish Chicken Bake

1 (6 ounce) package chicken stuffing mix	1 (170 g)
1⅔ cups water	410 ml
4 boneless, skinless chicken breast halves	4
1 (10 ounce) can cream of mushroom soup	1 (284 g)
⅓ cup sour cream	80 ml

1. Toss contents of vegetable-seasoning packet, stuffing mix and water and set aside.
2. Place chicken in greased 9 x 13-inch (23 x 33 cm) baking dish. Mix soup and sour cream in saucepan over low heat. Cook just enough to pour over chicken. Spoon stuffing evenly over top.
3. Bake uncovered at 375° (190° C) for 40 minutes.

~Great Served With~
Garlic-Green Beans-101 • Luscious Strawberry Salad-120

Tangy Chicken

1 (2 pound) broiler-fryer chicken, cut up	**1 (1 kg)**
3 tablespoons butter	**45 ml**
½ cup Heinz 57 sauce	**125 ml**
½ cup water	**125 ml**

1. Brown chicken pieces in skillet with butter. Place chicken pieces in shallow pan.
2. Combine sauce and water and pour over chicken. Cover with foil.
3. Bake at 350° (176° C) for 45 minutes. Remove foil last 10 minutes of cooking time so chicken can brown.

~Great Served With~
Creamy Mashed Potatoes-165
Broccoli-Cauliflower Salad-100

★

Curry-Glazed Chicken

3 tablespoons butter	**45 ml**
⅓ cup honey	**80 ml**
2 tablespoons dijon mustard	**30 ml**
1½ teaspoons curry powder	**7 ml**
4 boneless, skinless chicken breast halves	**4**

1. Place butter in 9 x 13-inch (23 x 33 cm) baking pan. Preheat oven to 375° (190° C) and melt butter.
2. Mix honey, mustard and curry powder in pan with butter. Add chicken to pan and turn mixture until chicken is coated.
3. Bake uncovered for 50 minutes and baste twice. Serve over rice.

~Great Served With~
Broccoli-Waldorf Salad-99 • Vegetable-Corn Medley-143

Honey-Baked Chicken

2 chickens, quartered	2
½ cup (1 stick) butter, melted	125 ml
⅔ cup honey	160 ml
¼ cup dijon mustard	60 ml
1 teaspoon curry powder	5 ml

1. Place chicken pieces in a large shallow baking dish, skin side up and sprinkle a little salt over chicken pieces.
2. Combine butter, honey, mustard and curry powder.
3. Pour over chicken, bake uncovered at 350° (176° C) for 1 hour 15 minutes and baste every 20 minutes.

~Great Served With~
Broccoli Supreme-148 • Sunflower Salad-103

Sweet and Sour Chicken

6 to 8 boneless, skinless chicken breast halves	6 to 8
Oil	
1 (1 ounce) package dry onion soup mix	1 (28 g)
1 (6 ounce) can frozen orange juice concentrate, thawed	1 (170 g)
⅔ cup water	160 ml

1. Brown chicken in a little oil or butter. Place chicken in greased 9 x 13-inch (23 x 33 cm) baking dish.
2. In small bowl, combine onion soup mix, orange juice and water and mix well. Pour over chicken.
3. Bake uncovered at 350° (176° C) for 45 to 50 minutes.

~Great Served With~
Mixed Vegetables and Cheese Casserole-162
Divinity Salad-122

Bacon-Wrapped Chicken

6 boneless, skinless chicken breast halves	**6**
1 (8 ounce) carton whipped cream cheese	
with onion and chives	**1 (228 g)**
Butter	
6 bacon strips	**6**

1. Flatten chicken to ½-inch (1 cm) thickness. Spread 3 tablespoons cream cheese over each piece. Dot with butter and a little salt and roll up. Wrap each with bacon strip. Place seam side down in greased 9 x 13-inch (23 x 33 cm) baking dish.
2. Bake uncovered at 375° (190° C) for 40 to 45 minutes or until juices run clear.
3. To brown, broil 6 inches (15 cm) from heat for about 3 minutes or until bacon is crisp.

~Great Served With~
Creamed Green Peas-154 • Special Rice Salad-111

Oregano Chicken

¼ cup (½ stick) butter, melted	**60 ml**
1 (1 ounce) envelope Italian salad dressing mix	**1 (28 g)**
2 tablespoons lemon juice	**30 ml**
4 boneless, skinless chicken breast halves	**4**
2 tablespoons dried oregano	**30 ml**

1. Combine butter, salad dressing mix and lemon juice. Place chicken in ungreased 9 x 13-inch (23 x 33 cm) baking pan. Spoon butter mixture over chicken.
2. Cover and bake at 350° (176° C) for 45 minutes. Uncover and baste with pan drippings and sprinkle with oregano.
3. Bake another 15 minutes longer or until chicken juices run clear.

~Great Served With~
Winter Salad-102 • Green Rice and Spinach-160

Oven-Fried Chicken

⅔ cup fine, dry breadcrumbs	160 ml
⅓ cup grated parmesan cheese	80 ml
½ teaspoon garlic salt	2 ml
6 boneless, skinless chicken breast halves	6
¼ cup Italian salad dressing	60 ml

1. In small bowl, combine breadcrumbs, cheese and garlic salt. Dip chicken in salad dressing, then dredge in crumb mixture. Place chicken in 9 x 13-inch (23 x 33 cm) sprayed pan.
2. Bake uncovered at 350° (176° C) for 50 minutes.

~Great Served With~
Baked Tomatoes-160 • Spinach-Apple Salad-105

Party Chicken Breasts

6 to 8 boneless, skinless chicken breast halves	6 to 8
8 strips bacon	8
1 (2.5 ounce) jar dried beef	1 (74 g)
1 (10 ounce) can cream of chicken soup	1 (284 g)
1 (8 ounce) carton sour cream	1 (228 g)

1. Wrap each chicken breast with strip of bacon and secure with toothpicks. Place dried beef in bottom of large, shallow baking pan and top with chicken.
2. Heat soup and sour cream, just enough to pour over chicken.
3. Bake uncovered at 325° (163° C) for 1 hour.

~Great Served With~
Almond-Green Beans-144 • Terrific Tortellini Salad-110

Fruited Chicken

6 large boneless, skinless, chicken breast halves	**6**
½ cup (1 stick) butter, melted	**125 ml**
⅔ cup flour	**160 ml**
1 (15 ounce) can chunky fruit cocktail with juice	**1 (438 g)**
Salt, pepper and paprika	

1. Dip chicken in butter and in flour. Place in 9 x 13-inch (23 x 33 cm) shallow baking dish. Sprinkle with a little salt, pepper and paprika.
2. Bake uncovered at 350° (176° C) for 45 minutes.
3. Pour fruit and half juice over chicken. Bake another 20 minutes.

~Great Served With~
Special Rice Salad-111 • Vegetable-Corn Medley-143

Picante Chicken

4 boneless, skinless chicken breast halves	**4**
1 (16 ounce) jar salsa	**1 (454 g)**
4 tablespoons brown sugar	**60 ml**
1 tablespoon prepared mustard	**15 ml**
Hot cooked rice	

1. Place chicken in sprayed shallow baking dish.
2. In a small bowl, combine salsa, brown sugar and mustard and pour over chicken.
3. Bake uncovered at 375° (190° C) for 45 minutes or until chicken juices run clear. Serve over rice.

~Great Served With~
City Slicker Salad-106 • Green Chili-Corn Casserole-143

Ranch Chicken

8 to 9 (2 pounds) chicken drumsticks	8 to 9
½ cup (1 stick) butter, melted	125 ml
½ cup parmesan cheese	125 ml
1½ cups corn flakes	375 ml
1 (1 ounce) package dry ranch-style dressing mix	1 (28 g)

1. Dip washed, dried chicken in melted butter. Combine cheese, corn flakes and dressing mix and dredge chicken in mixture.
2. Bake uncovered at 350° (176° C) for 50 minutes or until golden.

~Great Served With~
Scalloped Potatoes-167 • Broccoli-Noodle Salad-99

Cranberry Chicken

6 boneless, skinless chicken breasts halves	6
1 (16 ounce) can whole cranberry sauce	1 (454 g)
1 large tart apple, peeled, chopped	1
⅓ cup chopped walnuts	80 ml
1 teaspoon curry powder	5 ml

1. Place chicken in sprayed 9 x 13-inch (23 x 33 cm) baking pan. Bake uncovered at 350° (176° C) for 20 minutes.
2. Combine remaining ingredients and spoon over chicken.
3. Bake uncovered 25 minutes longer or until chicken juices run clear.

~Great Served With~
Garlic-Green Beans-101 • Marinated Corn Salad-107

Roasted Chicken and Vegetables

3 pounds chicken parts	1.5 kg
1 cup lemon pepper marinade with lemon juice, divided	250 ml
1 (16 ounce) package frozen mixed vegetables, thawed	1 (454 g)
¼ cup olive oil	60 ml
1 tablespoon seasoned salt	15 ml

1. Spray baking pan with non-stick vegetable spray. Arrange chicken skin-side down in pan. Pour ⅔ cup (160 ml) marinade over chicken. Bake uncovered at 375° (190° C) for 30 minutes.
2. Turn chicken over and baste with remaining ⅓ cup (80 ml) marinade.
3. Toss vegetables with oil and seasoned salt. Arrange vegetables around chicken and cover with foil. Return pan to oven and bake another 30 minutes.

~Great Served With~
Herbed New Potatoes-171 • Frozen Cherry Salad-126

Maple-Plum Glazed Turkey Breast

1 cup red plum jam	250 ml
1 cup maple syrup	250 ml
1 teaspoon dry mustard	5 ml
¼ cup lemon juice	60 ml
1 (5 pound) bone-in turkey breast	1 (2.5 kg)

1. In saucepan, combine plum jam, syrup, mustard and lemon. Bring to boiling point, turn heat down and simmer for about 20 minutes or until thick. Reserve 1 cup (250 ml).
2. Place turkey breast in roasting pan and pour remaining glaze over turkey. Bake according to directions on turkey breast.
3. Slice turkey and serve with heated reserved glaze.

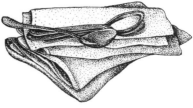

~Great Served With~
Frozen Cranberry-Pineapple Salad-126
Cheesy Green Beans-145

Beef Picante Skillet

1 pound lean ground beef	454 g
1 (10 ounce) can tomato soup	1 (284 g)
1 cup chunky salsa	250 ml
6 (6 inch) flour tortillas, cut into 1-inch pieces	6 (15 cm)
1¼ cups shredded cheddar cheese	310 ml

1. Cook beef in skillet until brown and pour off fat.
2. Add soup, salsa, ¾ cup (180 ml) water, tortillas, ½ teaspoon (2 ml) salt and half cheese. Heat to a boil. Cover and cook over low heat 5 minutes.
3. Top with remaining cheese. Serve right from skillet.

~Great Served With~
Sunny Yellow Squash-153 • Marinated Black-Eyed Peas-102

Spiced Beef

1 pound lean ground beef	454 g
1 (1.25 ounce) package taco seasoning mix	1 (32 g)
1 (16 ounce) can Mexican stewed tomatoes	
with liquid	1 (454 g)
1 (16 ounce) can kidney beans with liquid	1 (454 g)
1 (1 pound) bag egg noodles	1 (454 g)

1. Cook beef in skillet and drain. Add taco seasoning and ½ cup (125 ml) water. Simmer 15 minutes.
2. Add stewed tomatoes and kidney beans. (Add ¼ teaspoon (1 ml) salt if you like.)
3. Cook egg noodles according to package directions. Serve spiced beef over noodles.

~Great Served With~
Pineapple Slaw-108

Asian Beef and Noodles

1¼ pounds ground beef	310 ml
2 (3 ounce) packages oriental flavor instant Ramen noodles	2 (85 g)
1 (16 ounce) package frozen oriental stir-fry mixture	1 (454 g)
½ teaspoon ground ginger	2 ml
3 tablespoons thinly sliced, green onions	45 ml

1. In large skillet, brown ground beef and drain. Add ½ cup (125 ml) water, salt and pepper and simmer 10 minutes. Transfer to a separate bowl.
2. In same skillet, combine 2 cups (500 ml) water, vegetables, noodles (broken up), ginger and both seasoning packets. Bring to a boil, reduce heat. Cover, simmer 3 minutes or until noodles are tender and stir occasionally.
3. Return beef to skillet, and stir in green onions. Serve right from skillet.

~Great Served With~
Spinach-Apple Salad-105

Pinto Bean Pie

1 pound lean ground beef	**454 g**
1 onion, chopped	**1**
2 (16 ounce) cans pinto beans with liquid	**2 (454 g)**
1 (10 ounce) can tomatoes and green chilies	
with liquid	**1 (284 g)**
1 (6 ounce) can french-fried onion rings	**1 (170 g)**

1. In skillet, brown beef and onion and drain.
2. In 2-quart (2 L) casserole dish, layer 1 can beans, beef-onion mixture and one-half can tomatoes and green chilies. Repeat layer.
3. Top with onion rings and bake, uncovered at 350° (176° C) for 30 minutes.

~Great Served With~
Chili-Cheese Squash152 • Easy Guacamole Salad-110

Chili Casserole

1 (40 ounce) can chili with beans	**1 (1 kg)**
1 (4 ounce) can chopped green chilies	**1 (115 g)**
1 (2¼ ounce) can sliced ripe olives, drained	**1 (64 g)**
1 (8 ounce) package shredded cheddar cheese	**1 (228 g)**
2 cups ranch-flavored tortilla chips, crushed	**500 ml**

1. In bowl, combine all ingredients.
2. Transfer to greased 3-quart (3 L) casserole dish.
3. Bake, uncovered at 350° (176° C) for 35 minutes or until bubbly.

~Great Served With~
Red Hot Onions-112 • Shoe-Peg Corn-142

Chili Pie

2 cups small corn chips	500 ml
1 chopped onion	1
1 (19 ounce) can chili without beans	1 (550 g)
1½ cups grated cheddar cheese	375 ml

1. In 7 x 11-inch (18 x 28 cm) baking dish, place corn chips and top with onion, chili and cheese.
2. Bake at 350° (176° C) for about 15 minutes.

~Great Served With~
Baked Beans-163 • Calypso Coleslaw-109

Easy Chili

2 pounds lean ground chuck	1 kg
1 onion, chopped	1
4 (16 ounce) cans chili-hot beans with liquid	4 (454 g)
1 (1¾ ounce) packages chili seasoning mix	1 (30 g)
1 (46 ounce) can tomato juice	1 (1.3 kg)

1. Cook beef and onion in Dutch oven, stirring until meat crumbles and drain.
2. Stir in remaining ingredients.
3. Bring mixture to a boil, reduce heat and simmer, stirring occasionally for 2 hours.

~Great Served With~
Cornbread (with a Mix) • Broccoli-Noodle Salad-99

Corned Beef Supper

1 (4 to 5 pound) corned beef brisket	1 (2 to 2.5 kg)
4 large potatoes, peeled, quartered	4
6 carrots, peeled, halved	6
4 onions	4
1 head cabbage	1

1. Place corned beef in roaster and cover with water. Bring to a boil. Turn heat down and simmer 3 hours. Add water if necessary.
2. Add potatoes, carrots and onions. Cut cabbage into eighths and lay over top of other vegetables.
3. Bring to a boil, turn heat down and cook another 30 to 40 minutes until vegetables are done. When slightly cool, slice corned beef across grain.

~Great Served With~
Cornbread (with a Mix) • Fantastic Fruit Salad-114

Oven Brisket

1 (5 to 6) pound trimmed brisket	1 (2.5 to 3 kg)
1 (1 ounce) package onion soup mix	1 (28 g)
1 (12 ounce) can Coke (not diet)	1 (340 g)
1 (10 ounce) bottle Heinz 57 sauce	1 (284 g)

1. Place brisket, fat side up, in roasting pan.
2. In a bowl, combine onion mix, Coke and Heinz 57 sauce and pour over brisket. Cover and cook at 325° (163° C) for 4 to 5 hours or until tender. Remove brisket from pan and pour off drippings. Chill both, separately, overnight.
3. The next day, trim all fat from meat, slice and reheat. Skim fat off drippings and reheat. Serve sauce over brisket.

Smoked Brisket

1 (5 to 6 pound) trimmed brisket	1 (2.5 to 3 kg)
1 (6 ounce) bottle liquid smoke	1 (228 g)
Garlic and celery salt	
1 onion, chopped	1
Worcestershire sauce	
1 (6 ounce) bottle barbecue sauce	1 (170 g)

1. Place brisket in roasting pan. Pour liquid smoke over brisket. Sprinkle with garlic and celery salt and top with onion. Cover and refrigerate overnight.
2. Before cooking, pour off liquid smoke and douse with worcestershire.
3. Cover with foil and bake at 300° (149 ° C) for 5 hours. Uncover and pour barbecue sauce over brisket and bake 1 hour.

~Great Served With~
Baked Beans-163 • Broccoli-Waldorf Salad-99

Oven Brisket (p. 202)

~Great Served With~
Loaded Baked Potatoes-166
Broccoli-Cauliflower Salad-100

Great Brisket

2 onions, sliced	2
Paprika	
Seasoned salt	
1 (5 to 6 pound) trimmed brisket	1 (2.5 to 3 kg)
1 (12 ounce) Pepsi-Cola	1 (340 g)

1. Place onions in bottom of roasting pan. Sprinkle with paprika and seasoned salt. Lay brisket on top of onions and sprinkle more seasoned salt.
2. Bake, uncovered, at 450° (232 ° C) for 30 minutes. Pour Pepsi over roast and reduce oven to 325° (163 ° C). Cover with foil and bake until tender, about 4 hours or until tender.
3. Baste occasionally with Pepsi and juices from brisket.

~Great Served With~
Twice-Baked Potatoes-168 • Green Pea Salad-103

Sweet and Savory Brisket

1 (3 to 4 pound) trimmed beef brisket, halved	1 (1.5 to 2 kg)
¾ cup grape or plum jelly	375 ml
1 cup ketchup	250 ml
1 (1 ounce) envelope onion soup mix	1 (28 g)
¾ teaspoon black pepper	4 ml

1. Place half brisket in slow cooker. In bowl, combine jelly, ketchup, soup mix and pepper. Spread half over meat.
2. Top with remaining brisket and ketchup mixture. Cover and cook on low for 8 to 10 hours or until meat is tender.
3. Slice brisket and serve with cooking juices.

Heavenly Smoked Brisket

½ cup packed dark brown sugar	125 ml
2 tablespoons cajun seasoning	30 ml
1 tablespoon lemon pepper	15 ml
1 tablespoon worcestershire sauce	15 ml
1 (5 to 6 pound) beef brisket, untrimmed	1 (2.5 to 3 kg)

1. Combine sugar, cajun seasoning, pepper and worcestershire in shallow dish. Add brisket and turn to coat both sides. Cover and chill 8 hours.
2. Soak hickory wood chunks in water for 1 hour. Prepare charcoal fire in smoker and burn 20 minutes. Drain chunks and place on coals. Place water pan in smoker and add water to depth of fill line.
3. Remove brisket from marinade; place on lower food rack. Pour remaining marinade over meat. Cover with smoker lid. Cook 5 hours or until meat thermometer inserted in thickest portion registers 170° (80 ° C).

~Great Served With~
Broccoli-Cheese Potato Topper-167 • Nutty Green Salad-105

Sweet and Savory Brisket
(p. 204)

~Great Served With~
Macaroni, Cheese and Tomatoes-172
Easy Guacamole Salad-110

Lemon-Herb Pot Roast

1 (3 to 3½ pound) boneless beef chuck roast	**1 (1.5 to 2 kg)**
1 teaspoon garlic powder	**5 ml**
2 teaspoons lemon pepper	**10 ml**
1 teaspoon dried basil	**5 ml**
1 tablespoon oil	**15 ml**

1. Combine garlic, lemon pepper and basil and press evenly into surface of beef.
2. In Dutch oven, heat oil over medium-high heat and brown roast.
3. Add 1 cup (250 ml) water, bring to a boil and reduce heat to low. Cover tightly and simmer for 3 hours. Vegetables may be added to roast in last hour of cooking.

~Great Served With~
Marinated Corn Salad-107 • Frozen Cherry Salad-126

Prime Rib of Beef (p. 207)

~Great Served With~
Chive-Potato Souffle-169 • City Slicker Salad-106

Potato-Beef Casserole

4 medium potatoes, peeled, sliced	4
1¼ pounds lean ground beef, browned, drained	630 g
1 (10 ounce) can cream of mushroom soup	1 (284 g)
1 (10 ounce) can condensed vegetable beef soup	1 (284 g)
½ teaspoon salt, ½ teaspoon pepper	2 ml

1. In large bowl, combine all ingredients. Transfer to greased 3-quart (3 L) baking dish.
2. Bake covered at 350° (176° C) for 1 hour 30 minutes or until potatoes are tender.

~Great Served With~
Marinated Cucumbers-111 • Cheesy Green Beans-145

Prime Rib of Beef

⅓ cup each chopped onion and celery	80 ml
1 teaspoon salt	5 ml
½ teaspoon garlic powder	2 ml
1 (6 to 8 pound) beef rib roast	1 (3 to 4 kg)
1 (14 ounce) can beef broth	1 (420 g)

1. Combine onion and celery and place in greased roasting pan. Combine salt, garlic powder and a little black pepper and rub over roast. Place fat side up over vegetables.
2. Bake uncovered at 350° (176° C) for 2½ to 3½ hours or until meat reaches desired doneness. (Medium-rare is 140° (58° C); medium is 160° (70° C); well done is 170° (180° C).)
3. Let stand for about 15 minutes before carving. Skim fat from pan drippings and add beef broth. Stir to remove browned bits and heat. Strain and discard vegetables. Serve au jus with roast.

Savory Rib Roast

1 tablespoon dried thyme	15 ml
1 teaspoon dried rosemary, crushed	5 ml
1 teaspoon rubbed sage	5 ml
1 teaspoon pepper	5 ml
1 (6 pound) beef rib roast	1 (170 g)

1. In small bowl, combine thyme, rosemary, sage and pepper and rub over roast.
2. Place roast, fat side up, on rack in large roasting pan.
3. Bake uncovered at 350° (176° C) for 2 to 2½ hours or until meat reaches desired doneness. (Rare is 140° (58° C); medium is 160° (70° C); and well done is 170° (80° C).) Remove roast to a warm serving platter; let stand 10 minutes before slicing.

~Great Served With~
Creamed Spinach Bake-158 • Winter Salad-102

Shepherd's Pie

1 pound lean ground beef	454 g
1 (1 ounce) envelope taco seasoning mix	1 (28 g)
1 cup shredded cheddar cheese	250 ml
1 (11 ounce) can whole kernel corn, drained	1 (312 g)
2 cups mashed potatoes (use instant)	500 ml

1. In skillet, brown beef, cook 10 minutes and drain. Add taco seasoning and ¾ cup (180 ml) water and cook another 5 minutes.
2. Spoon beef mixture into 8-inch (20 cm) baking pan. Sprinkle cheese on top, then corn. Spread mashed potatoes over top.
3. Bake at 350° (176° C) for 25 minutes or until top is golden.

~Great Served With~
Broccoli-Cauliflower Salad-100 • Cinnamon Apple Salad-125

Delicious Meat Loaf

1½ pounds lean ground beef	680 g
⅔ cup Italian-seasoned dry breadcrumbs	160 ml
2 eggs, beaten	2
1 (10 ounce) can golden mushroom soup	1 (284 g)
2 tablespoons (¼ stick) butter	30 ml

1. Mix beef, breadcrumbs, half mushroom soup and eggs thoroughly. In baking pan, shape firmly into 8 x 4-inch (20 x 10 cm) loaf.
2. Bake at 350° (176° C) for 45 minutes.
3. In small saucepan, mix 2 tablespoons (30 ml) butter, remaining soup and ¼ cup (60 ml) water and heat thoroughly. Serve with meat loaf.

~Great Served With~
Mixed Vegetables and Cheese Casserole-162
Marinated Black-Eyed Peas-102

Spanish Meatloaf

1½ pounds lean ground beef	680 g
1 (16 ounce) can Spanish rice	1 (454 g)
1 egg, beaten	1
¾ cup round buttery cracker crumbs	180 ml
Chunky salsa	

1. Combine beef, rice, egg and crumbs. Shape into loaf in greased pan.
2. Bake at 350° (176° C) for 1 hour.
3. Serve with salsa on top of meat loaf.

~Great Served With~
Super Corn Casserole-142 • Marinated Cucumbers-111

Reuben Dogs

1 (27 ounce) can sauerkraut, rinsed, drained	1 (770 g)
2 teaspoons caraway seeds	10 ml
8 hot dogs, halved lengthwise	8
1 cup shredded Swiss cheese	250 ml
Thousand Island salad dressing	

1. Place sauerkraut in greased 2-quart (2 L) baking dish. Sprinkle with caraway seeds and top with hot dogs.
2. Bake uncovered at 350° (176° C) for 20 minutes or until heated through.
3. Sprinkle with cheese. Bake 3 to 5 minutes longer or until cheese melts. Serve with salad dressing.

~Great Served With~
Baked Beans-163 • Serendipity Salad-121

Pineapple-Pork Chops

6 to 8 thick boneless pork chops	6 to 8
1 (6 ounce) can frozen pineapple juice concentrate, thawed	1 (170 g)
3 tablespoons brown sugar	45 ml
⅓ cup wine or tarragon vinegar	80 ml
⅓ cup honey	80 ml

1. Place pork chops in a skillet in little oil and brown. (I like to buy boneless pork chops). Remove to shallow baking dish.
2. Combine pineapple juice, sugar, vinegar and honey. Pour over pork chops.
3. Cook covered at 325° (163° C) for about 50 minutes. Serve over hot rice.

~Great Served With~
Green and Red Salad-107 • Cauliflower Medley-151

Orange-Pork Chops

6 to 8 medium thick pork chops	6 to 8
Flour	
3 tablespoons butter	45 ml
2 cups orange juice	500 ml

1. Dip pork chops in flour and brown in skillet with butter. Place chops in 9 x 13-inch (23 x 33 cm) baking pan and pour remaining butter over top of pork chops.
2. Pour orange juice over chops.
3. Cover and bake at 325° (163° C) for 55 minutes. Uncover for last 15 minutes. Good served over hot rice.

~Great Served With~
Pine Nut Green Beans-146 • Sunflower Salad-103

Good
1.5.01

Oven-Pork Chops

6 to 8 medium-thick pork chops	6 to 8
1 (10 ounce) can cream of chicken soup	1 (284 g)
3 tablespoons ketchup	45 ml
1 tablespoon worcestershire	15 ml
1 medium onion, chopped	1

1. Brown pork chops in a little oil and season with salt and pepper. Place drained pork chops in a shallow baking dish.
2. In saucepan, combine soup, ketchup, worcestershire and onion. Heat just enough to mix and pour over pork chops.
3. Bake, covered at 350° (176° C) for 50 minutes. Uncover last 15 minutes.

~Great Served With~
Sunny Yellow Squash-153 • Broccoli-Waldorf Salad-99

Onion-Smothered Pork Chops

1 tablespoon oil	15 ml
6 (½-inch thick) pork chops	6 (1 cm)
1 onion, chopped	1
2 tablespoons butter	30 ml
1 (10 ounce) can cream of onion soup	1 (284 g)

1. In skillet, brown pork chops in oil and simmer about 10 minutes. Place pork chops in greased shallow baking pan.
2. In same skillet, add butter and saute chopped onion. (The pan juices will be brown from pork chops so onions will also be brown from those juices already in skillet.) Add onion soup and ¼ cup (60 ml) water and stir well. Sauce will have pretty light brown color.
3. Pour onion-soup mixture over pork chops. Cover and bake at 325° (163° C) for 40 minutes. Serve with brown rice.

~Great Served With~
Parmesan Broccoli-149 • Sunflower Salad-103

Mexicali-Pork Chops

1 (1 ounce) envelope taco seasoning	1 (28 g)
4 (½ inch thick) boneless pork loin chops	4 (1 cm)
1 tablespoon oil	15 ml
Salsa	

1. Rub taco seasoning over pork chops. In skillet, brown pork chops in oil over medium heat.
2. Add 2 tablespoons (30 ml) water, turn heat to low and simmer pork chops about 40 minutes. Add water if needed.
3. Spoon salsa over pork chops to serve.

~Great Served With~
Easy Guacamole Salad-110 • Shoe-Peg Corn-142

Pork Chops and Apples

6 thick-cut pork chops	6
Four	
Oil	
3 baking apples	3

1. Dip pork chops in flour and coat well. In skillet, brown pork chops in oil and place in 9 x 13-inch (23 x 33 cm) greased casserole.
2. Add about ⅓ cup (80 ml) water to casserole. Cook covered at 325° (163° C) for about 50 minutes.
3. Peel, half and seed apples. Place ½ apple on top of each pork chop. Return to oven for about 10 minutes. (Don't overcook apples.)

Simple, easy and delicious!

~Great Served With~
Carnival Couscous-171 • Creamy Cranberry Salad-124

Pork Chops in Cream Gravy

4 (¼-inch thick) pork chops	**4 (.5 cm)**
Flour	
Oil	
2¼ cups whole milk	**560 ml**

1. Trim all fat off pork chops. Dip chops in flour with a little salt and pepper. Brown pork chops on both sides in a little oil. Remove chops from skillet.
2. Add about 2 tablespoons (30 ml) flour to skillet, brown lightly and stir in little salt and pepper. Slowly stir in milk to make gravy.
3. Return chops to skillet with gravy. Cover and simmer on low burner for about 40 minutes. Serve over rice or noodles.

Grilled Pork Loin

1 (4 pound) boneless pork loin roast	**1 (2 kg)**
1 (8 ounce) bottle Italian salad dressing	**1 (228 g)**
1 cup dry white wine	**250 ml**
3 cloves garlic, minced	**3**
10 black peppercorns	**10**

1. Pierce roast at 1-inch (2.5 cm) intervals with fork and set aside. (Piercing allows marinade to penetrate meat better.)
2. Combine salad dressing and remaining ingredients in large plastic bag. Reserve ½ cup (125 ml) mixture for basting during grilling. Add roast to remaining mixture in bag. Chill 8 hours and turn occasionally.
3. Remove roast from marinade and discard marinade. Place roast on rack in cooking grill. Cook, covered with grill lid, for 35 minutes or until meat thermometer inserted into thickest portion reaches 160° (70° C). Turn and baste with reserve ½ cup (125 ml) dressing mixture.

Apricot-Baked Ham

1 (12 to 20 pound) whole ham, fully cooked	1 (6 to 10 kg)
Whole cloves	
2 tablespoons dry mustard	30 ml
1¼ cups apricot jam	310 ml
1¼ cups packed light brown sugar	310 ml

1. Heat oven to 450° (232° C). Place ham on rack in large roasting pan and insert cloves in ham every inch or so.
2. Combine dry mustard and jam. Spread over entire surface of ham. Pat brown sugar over jam mixture.
3. Reduce heat to 325° (163° C). Bake uncovered at 15 minutes per pound.

This is the ham you will want for Easter dinner!

~Great Served With~
Mixed Vegetables and Cheese Casseroles-162
Frozen Cranberry-Pineapple Salad-126

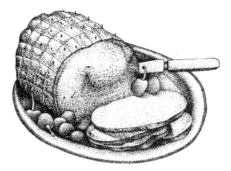

Grilled Pork Loin (p. 214)

~Great Served With~
Herbed New Potatoes-171 • Green Pea Salad-103

Baked Ham and Pineapple

1 (6 to 8 pound) fully cooked, bone-in ham	**1 (3 to 4 kg)**
Whole cloves	
½ cup packed brown sugar	**125 ml**
1 (8 ounce) can sliced pineapple with juice	**1 (228 g)**
5 maraschino cherries	**5**

1. Place ham in roasting pan. Score surface with shallow diagonal cuts, making diamond shapes and insert cloves into diamonds. Cover and bake at 325° (163° C) for 1½ hours.
2. Combine brown sugar and juice from can of pineapple and pour over ham. Arrange pineapple slices and cherries on ham.
3. Bake uncovered 40 minutes longer.

~Great Served With~
Green Rice and Spinach-160 • Cherry-Cranberry Salad-123

Praline Ham

2 (½ inch thick) ham slices, cooked (about 2½ pounds)	**2 (1 cm)** **1 kg**
½ cup maple syrup	**125 ml**
3 tablespoons brown sugar	**45 ml**
1 tablespoon butter	**15 ml**
⅓ cup chopped pecans	**80 ml**

1. Bake ham slices in shallow pan at 325° (163° C) for 10 minutes.
2. Bring syrup, sugar and butter to boil in small saucepan and stir often. Stir in pecans and spoon over ham.
3. Bake another 20 minutes.

~Great Served With~
Carnival Couscous-171 • Marinated Corn Salad-107

Grilled Ham and Apples

½ cup orange marmalade	125 ml
2 teaspoons (¼ stick) butter	10 ml
¼ teaspoon ground ginger	1 ml
2 (½ inch thick) ham slices	2 (1 cm)
(about 2½ pounds)	1 kg
2 apples, quartered	2

1. Combine marmalade, butter and ginger in 1-cup (250 ml) glass measuring cup. Microwave on HIGH 1 minute or until mixture melts and stir once.
2. Cook ham covered with apples. Cover with grill lid and cook over medium hot coals. Turn occasionally and baste with marmalade mixture, about 20 minutes.

~Great Served With~
Loaded Baked Potatoes-166 • Broccoli-Cauliflower Salad-100

Peachy Glazed Ham

1 (15 ounce) can sliced peaches in light syrup	
with juice	1 (438 g)
2 tablespoons dark brown sugar	30 ml
2 teaspoons dijon mustard	10 ml
1 (1 pound) center-cut ham slice	1 (454 g)
⅓ cup sliced green onions	80 ml

1. Drain peaches and reserve ½ cup (125 ml) syrup in large skillet and set peaches aside.
2. Add sugar and mustard to skillet; bring to boil over medium high heat. Cook 2 minutes or until slightly reduced.
3. Add ham and cook 2 minutes on each side. Add peaches and green onions, cover and cook over low heat 3 minutes or until peaches are thoroughly heated.

~Great Served With~
Cauliflower Medley-151 • Broccoli-Noodle Salad-99

Ham with Orange Sauce

1 (½ inch thick) slice fully cooked ham	1 (1 cm)
1 cup orange juice	250 ml
2 tablespoons brown sugar	30 ml
1½ tablespoons cornstarch	22 ml
⅓ cup golden raisins	80 ml

1. Place ham slice in shallow baking dish.
2. In a saucepan, combine orange juice, brown sugar, cornstarch and raisins. Bring to a boil, stirring constantly, until mixture thickens slightly. Pour over ham slice.
3. Warm at 350° (176° C) for about 20 minutes.

~Great Served With~
Creamy Vegetable Casserole-163 • Divinity Salad-122

Pineapple Sauce for Ham

Pre-sliced, cooked honey-baked ham slices	
1 (15 ounce) can pineapple chunks with juice	1 (438 g)
1 cup apricot preserves	250 ml
1¼ cups packed brown sugar	310 ml
¼ teaspoon cinnamon	1 ml

1. Place ham slices in shallow baking pan. In saucepan, combine pineapple, preserves, brown sugar and cinnamon and heat.
2. Pour sauce over ham slices

~Great Served With~
Mediterranean Potato Salad-108 • Asparagus Bake-140

Orange Sauce for Ham

⅔ cup orange juice	160 ml
⅓ cup water	80 ml
2 tablespoons brown sugar	30 ml
1½ tablespoons cornstarch	22 ml
⅓ cup golden raisins	80 ml

1. Mix all ingredients in saucepan.
2. Heat and cook, stirring constantly, until sauce thickens and is clear and bubbly.
3. Serve with pre-cooked ham.

Dijon Baby-Back Ribs

4 pounds baby back pork ribs	2 kg
1 (12 ounce) bottle dijon-honey marinade with lemon juice, divided	1 (340 g)

1. If needed, cut ribs in lengths to fit in large, resealable plastic bag. Place ribs in bag and add ¾ cup (180 ml) marinade. Seal bag and shake to coat. Marinate in refrigerator overnight.
2. Discard used marinade and place ribs on sprayed broiler pan.
3. Bake uncovered at 300° (149° C) for about 2 hours. Finish browning and cooking on grill, basting often with remaining marinade.

Tangy Apricot Ribs

3 to 4 pounds baby-back pork loin ribs	1.5 to 2 kg
1 (16 ounce) jar apricot preserves	1 (454 g)
⅓ cup soy sauce	80 ml
¼ cup packed light brown sugar	60 ml
2 teaspoons garlic powder	10 ml

1. Place ribs in large roasting pan. Whisk preserves and soy sauce, brown sugar and garlic powder until blended. Pour over ribs, cover and chill overnight.
2. Remove ribs from marinade and reserve marinade in small saucepan. Line baking pan with foil, add ribs and sprinkle a little salt and pepper.
3. Bring marinade to a boil, cover, reduce heat and simmer 5 minutes. Bake ribs at 325° (163° C) for 1 hour 30 minutes or until tender and baste frequently with marinade.

~Great Served With~
Scalloped Potatoes-167 • Broccoli-Waldorf Salad-99

Sweet and Sour Spareribs

3 to 4 pounds spareribs	1.5 to 2 kg
3 tablespoons soy sauce	45 ml
⅓ cup prepared mustard	80 ml
1 cup packed brown sugar	250 ml
½ teaspoon garlic salt	2 ml

1. Place spareribs in roasting pan. Bake at 325° (163° C) for 45 minutes and drain.
2. Make sauce with remaining ingredients and brush on ribs.
3. Return to oven, reduce heat to 300° (149° C) and bake for 1 hour or until tender. Baste several times while cooking.

~Great Served With~
Creamy Mashed Potatoes-165 • Broccoli-Noodle Salad-99

Spunky Spareribs

5 to 6 pounds spareribs	2.5 to 3 kg
1 (6 ounce) can frozen orange juice	1(170 g)
2 teaspoons worcestershire sauce	10 ml
½ teaspoon garlic powder	2 ml

1. Place spareribs in shallow baking pan, meat side down. Sprinkle with a little salt and pepper. Roast at 375° (190° C) for 30 minutes. Turn ribs and roast another 15 minutes and drain fat.
2. Combine remaining ingredients and brush mixture on ribs.
3. Reduce heat to 300° (149° C). Cover ribs and roast 2 hours or until tender and baste occasionally.

~Great Served With~
Twice-Baked Potatoes-168 • Winter Salad-102

Italian Sausage and Ravioli

1 pound sweet Italian pork sausage, casing removed	454 g
1 (1 pound, 10-ounce jar) extra chunky mushroom and green pepper spaghetti sauce	740 g
1 (24 ounce) package frozen cheese-filled ravioli, cooked, drained	1 (680 g)
Grated parmesan cheese	

1. In very large skillet over medium heat, cook sausage until brown and no longer pink. Stir to separate sausage or slice sausage and drain.
2. Stir in spaghetti sauce and heat to boiling. Cook ravioli as package directs and add to spaghetti and sausage.
3. Sprinkle with parmesan cheese. Pour into serving dish.

~Great Served With~
Nutty Green Salad-105

Baked Applesauce

5 pounds tart green apples, peeled, cored, sliced 2.5 kg
1 (8 ounce) jar plum jelly 1 (228 g)
½ cup sugar 125 ml
⅓ cup lemon juice 80 ml
¼ teaspoon ground nutmeg 1 ml

1. Place apples in 2-quart (2 L) casserole. In saucepan, combine jelly, sugar and ⅔ cup (160 ml) water. Heat until jelly melts. Remove from heat, stir in lemon juice and nutmeg and pour over apples.
2. Bake covered at 350° (176° C) for 1 hour 15 minutes or until apples are soft. Delicious served with pork.

Cranberries and Apples

2 (21 ounce) cans pie apples 2 (600 g)
1 (16 ounce) can whole cranberry sauce 1 (454 g)
2 cups sugar 500 ml
1 teaspoon ground cinnamon 5 ml
Red food coloring, optional

1. In large saucepan, mix apples, cranberry sauce, sugar and cinnamon. Add a few drops of red coloring.
2. Simmer for about 45 minutes, stir occasionally and chill.
3. Great served with pork.

Orange Roughy with Peppers

1 pound orange roughy	454 ml
1 onion, sliced	1
2 red bell peppers, cut into julienne strips	2
1 teaspoon dried thyme leaves	5 ml
¼ teaspoon black pepper	1 ml

1. Cut fish into 4-serving pieces. Heat a little oil in a skillet. Layer onion and bell peppers and sprinkle with half thyme and pepper.
2. Place fish over peppers and sprinkle with remaining thyme and pepper.
3. Turn burner on high until fish is hot enough to cook. Lower heat, cover and cook fish for 15 to 20 minutes or until fish flakes easily.

~Great Served With~
Creamy Vegetable Casserole-163 • Sunflower Salad-103

Lemon-Dill Fish

½ cup mayonnaise	**125 ml**
2 tablespoons lemon juice	**30 ml**
½ teaspoon lemon peel	**2 ml**
1 teaspoon dill weed	**5 ml**
1 pound cod or flounder fillets	**454 g**

1. Combine mayonnaise, lemon juice, peel and dill weed until well blended.
2. Place fish on greased grill or broiler rack. Brush with half sauce. Grill or broil 5 to 8 minutes, turn and brush with remaining sauce.
3. Continue grilling or broiling 5 to 8 minutes or until fish flakes easily with fork.

~Great Served With~
Asparagus Bake-140 • Broccoli-Noodle Salad-99

Flounder Au Gratin

½ cup fine dry breadcrumbs	**125 ml**
¼ cup grated parmesan cheese	**60 ml**
1 pound flounder	**454 g**
⅓ cup mayonnaise	**80 ml**

1. In shallow dish combine crumbs and cheese. Brush both sides of fish with mayonnaise. Coat with crumb mixture.
2. Arrange in single layer in shallow pan.
3. Bake at 375° (190° C) for 20 to 25 minutes or until fish flakes easily.

~Great Served With~
Broccoli-Stuffed Tomatoes-150 • Scalloped Potatoes-167

Baked Fish

1 pound fish filets	454 g
Sauce: 3 tablespoons butter	45 ml
1 teaspoon tarragon	5 ml
2 teaspoons capers	10 ml
2 tablespoons lemon juice	30 ml

1. Place fish filets in greased shallow pan. Sprinkle with salt, pepper and a little butter. Bake at 375° (190° C) for about 8 to 10 minutes; turn and bake another 6 minutes or until fish flakes.
2. For sauce, melt butter with tarragon, capers and lemon juice. Serve over warm fish.

~Great Served With~
Carnival Couscous-171 • Creamy Orange Salad-114

Spicy Catfish Amandine

¼ cup (½ stick) butter, melted	60 ml
3 tablespoons lemon juice	45 ml
6 to 8 catfish fillets	6 to 8
1½ teaspoons creole seasoning	7 ml
½ cup sliced almonds	125 ml

1. Combine butter and lemon juice and dip each fillet in butter mixture. Arrange in 9 x 13-inch (23 x 33 cm) baking dish.
2. Sprinkle fish with creole seasoning.
3. Bake at 375° (190° C) for 25 to 30 minutes or until fish flakes easily when tested with fork. Sprinkle almonds over fish for last 5 minutes of baking.

~Great Served With~
Macaroni, Cheese and Tomatoes-172 • Pineapple Slaw-108

Golden Catfish Fillets

3 eggs	3
¾ cup flour	180 ml
¾ cup cornmeal	180 ml
1 teaspoon garlic powder	5 ml
6 to 8 (4 to 8 ounce) catfish fillets	6 to 8
	(115 to 228 g)

1. In shallow bowl, beat eggs until foamy. In another shallow bowl, combine flour, cornmeal, seasonings and a little salt.
2. Dip fillets in eggs and coat with cornmeal mixture.
3. Heat ¼-inch (.5 cm) oil in large skillet and fry fish over medium-high heat for about 4 minutes on each side or until fish flakes easily with fork.

~Great Served With~
Baked Beans-163 • Broccoli-Cauliflower Salad-100

Curried Red Snapper

1½ pounds fresh red snapper	680 ml
2 medium onions, chopped	2
2 celery ribs, chopped	2
1 teaspoon curry powder	5 ml
¼ cup milk	60 ml

1. Place snapper in greased 9 x 13-inch (23 x 33 cm) baking pan.
2. In skillet, saute onions and celery in little butter. Add curry powder and a little salt and mix well. Remove from heat and stir in milk. Spoon over snapper.
3. Bake uncovered at 350° (176° C) for 25 minutes or until fish flakes easily with fork.

~Great Served With~
Mixed Vegetables and Cheese Casserole-162
Serendipity Salad-121

Chipper Fish

2 pounds sole or orange roughy	1 kg
½ cup Caesar salad dressing	125 ml
1 cup crushed potato chips	250 ml
½ cup shredded cheddar cheese	125 ml

1. Dip fish in dressing and place in greased baking dish.
2. Combine chips and cheese and sprinkle over fish.
3. Bake at 375° (190° C) for about 20 to 25 minutes.

~Great Served With~
Almond-Green Beans-144 • Marinated Cucumbers-111

Shrimp Newburg

1 (10 ounce) can condensed	
cream of shrimp soup	1 (284 g)
¼ cup water	60 ml
1 teaspoon seafood seasoning	5 ml
1 (1 pound) package frozen cooked, salad	
shrimp, thawed	1 (454 g)

1. In saucepan, combine soup, water and seafood seasoning.
   Bring to a boil, reduce heat and stir in shrimp. Heat
   thoroughly and serve over hot white rice.

~Great Served With~
Spinach-Apple Salad-105 • Best Cauliflower-151

Shrimp Scampi

2 pounds raw shrimp, peeled	1 kg
½ cup (1 stick) butter	125 ml
3 cloves garlic, pressed	3
¼ cup lemon juice	60 ml
Hot sauce	

1. Melt butter, saute garlic and add lemon juice and a few dashes of hot sauce.
2. Arrange shrimp in single layer in shallow pan. Pour garlic-butter over shrimp and salt lightly.
3. Broil 2 minutes, turn shrimp and broil 2 more minutes. Reserve garlic-butter and serve separately.

~Great Served With~
Pine Nut Green Beans-146 • City Slicker Salad-106

Skillet-Shrimp Scampi

2 teaspoons olive oil	10 ml
2 pounds uncooked shrimp, peeled, veined	1 kg
⅔ cup herb-garlic marinade with lemon juice	160 ml
¼ cup finely chopped green onion with tops	160 ml

1. In large non-stick skillet, heat oil. Add shrimp and marinade.
2. Cook, stirring often, until shrimp turns pink. Stir in green onions.
3. Serve over hot, cooked rice or your favorite pasta.

~Great Served With~
Cheesy Green Beans-145 • Broccoli-Cauliflower Salad-100

Your Guide to Leftover Turkey, Chicken and Ham

Add 3 cups (750 ml) cubed chicken or turkey to Salads

Chicken or Turkey Salad With Relish

⅔ cup chopped celery	160 ml
¾ cup sweet pickle relish	180 ml
1 bunch fresh green onions with tops, chopped	1
3 hard-boiled eggs, chopped	3
¾ cup mayonnaise	180 ml

1. Combine 3 cups (750 ml) chopped chicken, celery, relish, onions and eggs.
2. Toss with mayonnaise and chill.
3. Serve on lettuce leaf.

Tropical Chicken or Turkey Salad

⅔ cup chopped celery	160 ml
⅔ cup toasted slivered almonds	160 ml
2 small, firm bananas, sliced	2
1 (8 ounce) can pineapple tidbits, drained	1 (228 g)
¾ cup mayonnaise	180 ml

1. Combine 3 cups (750 ml) chopped chicken, celery, almonds, bananas and pineapple and toss with mayonnaise.
2. Refrigerate. Serve on lettuce leaf.

Add 3 cups (750 ml) cubed chicken or turkey to Salads.

Chicken or Turkey Salad Potpourri

1 cup chopped celery	250 ml
1 cup tart green apple, peeled, cubed	250 ml
1 (10 ounce) can mandarin oranges, drained	1 (284 g)
¾ cup chopped macadamia nuts	180 ml
1 teaspoon curry powder,	5 ml
¾ cup mayonnaise	180 ml

1. Combine 3 cups (750 ml) chopped chicken, celery, apple, oranges and nuts.
2. Toss with curry powder and mayonnaise and chill.
3. Serve on lettuce leaf.

Chicken or Turkey Salad Mandarin

1 cup celery	250 ml
1½ cups green grapes, halved	375 ml
¾ cup cashew nuts	180 ml
¾ cup mayonnaise	180 ml
1 cup chow mein noodles	250 ml

1. Combine 3 cups (750 ml) chopped chicken, celery, grapes and cashew nuts and toss with mayonnaise. Just before serving, mix in noodles and serve on cabbage leaf.

Add 3 cups (750 ml) cubed chicken or turkey to Salads.

American Chicken or Turkey Salad

⅔ cup chopped celery,	160 ml
½ cup chopped pecans	125 ml
⅔ cup chopped sweet yellow bell pepper	160 ml
1 bunch fresh green onions with tops, chopped	1
⅔ cup pickle relish	160 ml
⅔ cup mayonnaise	160 ml

1. Combine 3 cups (750 ml) chopped chicken, celery, pecans, bell pepper, onions and relish and toss with mayonnaise.
2. Refrigerate and serve on shredded lettuce.

Chicken or Turkey Salad Crunch

⅔ cup celery	160 ml
1 (8 ounce) can sliced water chestnuts	1 (228 g)
1½ cups seedless red grapes, halved	375 ml
⅔ cup chopped pecans	160 ml
¾ cup mayonnaise,	180 ml
½ teaspoon curry powder	2 ml

1. Combine 3 cups (750 ml) chopped chicken, celery, water chestnuts, grapes and pecans.
2. Toss with mayonnaise and curry powder and serve on cabbage leaf.

Add 3 cups (750 ml) cubed chicken or turkey to Salads.

Wild Chicken or Turkey Salad

1 (6 ounce) box long-grain wild rice, cooked, drained	1 (170 g)
1 bunch fresh green onions with tops, chopped	1
1 cup chopped walnuts	250 ml
1 (8 ounce) can sliced water chestnuts	1 (228 g)
1 cup mayonnaise,	250 ml
¾ teaspoon curry powder	4 ml

1. Combine 3 cups (750 ml) chopped chicken, rice, onions, walnuts and water chestnuts.
2. Toss with mayonnaise and curry powder and chill.
3. Serve on bed of lettuce.

Colorful Chicken or Turkey Salad

⅔ cup chopped celery	160 ml
1 (15 ounce) can pineapple tidbits, drained	1 (438 g)
¾ cup slivered almonds, toasted	180 ml
¾ cup chopped red bell pepper	180 ml
⅔ cup mayonnaise	160 ml

1. Combine 3 cups (750 ml) chopped chicken, celery, pineapple, almonds and bell pepper and toss with mayonnaise and chill.
2. Serve on lettuce leaf.

Casseroles

Add 3 cups (750 ml) chopped chicken or turkey to Casseroles.

Chicken-Broccoli Casserole

1 (16 ounce) package frozen broccoli flowerets, thawed	1 (454 g)
1 (10 ounce) can cream of chicken soup, diluted with ¼ cup water	1 (284 g) 60 ml
⅔ cup mayonnaise	160 ml
1 cup shredded cheddar cheese	250 ml
1½ cups crushed cheese crackers	375 ml

1. Combine chicken, broccoli, soup, mayonnaise and cheese and mix well.
2. Pour into buttered 3-quart (3 L) casserole. Spread cheese crackers over top.
3. Bake uncovered at 350° (176° C) for 40 minutes.

Sherried-Chicken Casserole

1 (4 ounce) can sliced mushrooms, drained	1 (115 g)
1 (10 ounce) can cream of chicken soup, diluted with ¼ cup water	1 (284 g) 60 ml
1 (8 ounce) carton sour cream	1 (228 g)
⅓ cup cooking sherry	80 ml
1 (1 ounce) envelope dry onion soup mix	1 (28 g)

1. Combine chicken, mushrooms, soup, sour cream, sherry and onion soup mix.
2. Pour into buttered 3-quart (3 L) casserole.
3. Bake covered at 350° (176° C) for 40 minutes. Serve over hot white rice.

Add 3 cups (750 ml) chopped chicken or turkey to Casseroles.

Chicken-Green Peas Casserole

1 (6.9 ounce) box chicken Rice-A-Roni	1 (190 g)
1 (10 ounce) can cream of mushroom soup	1 (284 g)
1 (10 ounce) can cream of celery soup	1 (284 g)
1 (10 ounce) package frozen green peas, thawed	1 (284 g)
1 cup shredded cheddar cheese	250 ml

1. Cook Rice-A-Roni according to package directions.
2. Combine cooked rice, soups, peas, cheese and ½ cup (125 ml) water and mix well.
3. Pour into a buttered 3-quart (3 L) casserole and bake covered at 350° (176° C) for 40 minutes.

Chicken Casserole Pepe

1 (10 ounce) bag corn tortillas	1 (284 g)
1 onion, chopped	1
1 (10 ounce) can cream of chicken soup	1 (284 g)
2 (10 ounce) cans tomatoes and green chilies	2 (284 g)
1 (16 ounce) package cubed processed cheese	1 (454 g)

1. Place half corn tortillas in non-stick vegetable sprayed 9 x 13-inch (23 x 33 cm) baking dish and crush with palm. In large saucepan, combine onion, soup, tomatoes and cheese. Heat on medium and stir until cheese melts. Add 3 cups (750 ml) chicken and pour over corn tortillas.
2. Crush remaining corn tortillas in baggie with rolling pin. Sprinkle over chicken-cheese mixture.
3. Bake uncovered at 350° (176° C) about 40 minutes or until bubbly around edges.

Add 3 cups (750 ml) chopped chicken or turkey to Casseroles.

Curried Chicken Casserole

2 (10 ounce) cans cream of mushroom soup	2 (284 g)
1 soup can milk, 2 teaspoons curry powder	10 ml
1 (4 ounce) can sliced mushrooms, drained	1 (115 g)
2½ cups cooked instant rice	625 ml
3 cooked, crisp bacon slices, chopped	3

1. In large saucepan, combine 3 cups (750 ml) chicken and all remaining ingredients.
2. Pour into 9 x 13-inch (23 x 33 cm) non-stick vegetable-sprayed baking dish.
3. Bake covered at 350° (176° C) for 40 minutes.

Creamy Chicken Casserole

1 (10 ounce) can cream of celery soup	1 (284 g)
1 (8 ounce) carton sour cream	1 (228 g)
1 package dry onion soup mix	1 (28 g)
1 (8 ounce) can green peas, drained	1 (228 g)
2 cups cracker crumbs	500 ml

1. In large saucepan, combine 3 cups (750 ml) chicken, soup, sour cream and onion soup mix and heat just enough to mix well.
2. Add green peas and spoon into buttered 3-quart (3 L) baking dish. Sprinkle crumbs over top of casserole.
3. Bake uncovered at 350° (176° C) for 35 minutes or until bubbly.

Ham Salads

Add 3 cups (750 ml) chopped ham to Salads.

Relished-Ham Salad

½ cup chopped celery	125 ml
1 bunch fresh green onions with tops, chopped	1
⅓ cup sweet pickle relish	80 ml
1 teaspoon mustard,	5 ml
⅔ cup mayonnaise	160 ml
1 (1.5 ounce) can shoe-string potato sticks	1 (42 g)

1. Combine chopped ham, celery, onions and relish, toss with mustard and mayonnaise and chill.
2. When ready to serve, fold in potato sticks and serve on cabbage leaf.

Sunny Ham Salad

1 bunch fresh green onions with tops, chopped	1
½ cup toasted silvered almonds, toasted	125 ml
½ cup sunflower seeds	125 ml
2 cups chopped fresh broccoli flowerets	500 ml
¾ cup mayonnaise	180 ml

1. Combine chopped ham, green onions, almonds, sunflower seeds and broccoli flowerets, toss with mayonnaise and chill.
2. Serve on lettuce leaves.

Add 3 cups (750 ml) chopped ham to Salads.

Mexi-Ham Salad

1 (15 ounce) can pinto beans, drained	1 (438 g)
½ large purple onion, chopped	½
1 (11 ounce) can Mexi-corn, drained	1 (312 g)
1 cup chopped celery	250 ml
About ½ to ¾ (8 ounce) bottle Italian dressing	½ (228 g)

1. Combine chopped ham, beans, onion, corn and celery, toss with salad dressing and chill.
2. Serve on bed of shredded lettuce.

Crunchy Ham Salad

¾ cup chopped celery	180 ml
1 cup small-curd cottage cheese, drained	250 ml
1 cup cut-up cauliflower flowerets	250 ml
1 cup cut-up broccoli flowerets	250 ml
Prepared honey mustard dressing	

1. Combine chopped ham, celery, cottage cheese, cauliflower and broccoli, toss with dressing and chill.
2. Serve on lettuce leaves.

English Pea Ham Salad

⅔ cup chopped celery	160 ml
1 (15 ounce) can English peas, drained	1 (438 g)
1 red bell pepper, chopped	1
1 (8 ounce) package cubed mozzarella cheese	1 (228 g)
¾ cup Garlic-Mayonnaise (page 136)	180 ml

1. Combine ham, celery, peas, bell pepper and cheese, toss with garlic mayonnaise and chill.
2. Serve on cabbage leaves.

Casseroles

Use with leftover turkey, chicken or ham.

Chicken (or Turkey) Jambalaya

1 (15 ounce) can stewed tomatoes with liquid	1 (438 g)
1 (1 ounce) package dry vegetable soup-dip mix	1 (28 g)
¾ teaspoon crushed red pepper	4 ml
2 cups chopped chicken or turkey	500 ml
1 cup ham, cut into matchsticks	250 ml

1. In large skillet, combine tomatoes, 2 cups (500 ml) water, soup mix and red pepper. Bring to a boil and stir well.
2. Reduce heat, cover and simmer 15 minutes.
3. Stir in chicken or turkey and cook 5 minutes longer. Serve over hot white, cooked rice.

Turkey (or Chicken) and Dressing Pie

1 (6 ounce) box stuffing mix	1 (170 g)
3 tablespoons butter, melted	45 g
2½ cups finely chopped, cooked turkey or chicken	625 ml
1 cup shredded cheddar cheese	250 ml
4 eggs, beaten	4
2 cups half-and-half cream	500 ml

1. Combine dressing, seasoning packet and butter and mix well. Press on bottom and sides of buttered, 2-quart (2 L) baking dish. Bake at 400° (204° C) for 5 minutes and cool.
2. Combine turkey and cheese and spread over dressing mixture in pan. Combine eggs and half-and-half and beat well. Pour over turkey mixture.
3. Reduce oven to 325° (163° C). Bake uncovered for 35 to 40 minutes or until set.

Golden Chicken (or Turkey) Casserole

2½ cups cubed cooked chicken or turkey	625 ml
1 (8 ounce) can pineapple chunks or tidbits, drained	1 (228 g)
½ cup apricot preserves	125 ml
1 (10 ounce) can cream of chicken soup	1 (228 g)
1 (8 ounce) can sliced water chestnuts	1 (228 g)

1. In bowl, combine all ingredients, plus ⅓ cup (80 ml) water and mix well. Transfer to buttered 2-quart (2 L) baking dish.
2. Bake uncovered at 350° (176° C) for 35 minutes or until thoroughly heated.
3. Serve over hot cooked rice.

Ranch Pasta and Turkey (or Chicken)

1 (8 ounce) package of your favorite pasta	1 (228 g)
½ cup (1 stick) butter	125 ml
1 (1 ounce) envelope ranch-style dressing dry mix	1 (28 g)
1 (15 ounce) can peas and carrots with liquid	1 (438 g)
3 cups cubed turkey or chicken	750 ml

1. Cook pasta according to directions on package. In saucepan, combine butter, dressing mix, peas and carrots. Heat until butter melts.
2. Toss with pasta and turkey. Place in 2-quart (2 L) casserole.
3. Heat at 350° (176° C) for about 20 minutes. (Sprinkle grated cheese over top after casserole bakes if you like.)

Chicken-Broccoli Casserole

1 (10 ounce) can cream of chicken soup	**1 (284 g)**
¾ cup milk	**180 ml**
3 cups diced cooked chicken or turkey	**750 ml**
1 (10 ounce) box broccoli spears, thawed	**1 (284 g)**
1 (6 ounce) box chicken stuffing mix	**1 (170 g)**

1. Heat soup and milk, just enough to mix well. Pour into greased 9 x 13-inch (23 x 33 cm) baking dish.
2. Layer chicken over soup and place broccoli on top. Prepare stuffing mix according to package directions. Top with stuffing mix.
3. Bake covered at 350° (176° C) for 50 minutes.

Ham-Potato Casserole

1 (24 ounce) package frozen hash browns with onion and peppers	**1 (785 g)**
3 cups cooked, cubed ham	**750 ml**
1 (10 ounce) can cream of chicken soup	**1 (284 g)**
1 (10 ounce) can cream of celery soup	**1 (284 g)**
1 (8 ounce) package shredded cheddar cheese	**1 (228 g)**

1. In large bowl, combine hash browns, ham, chicken soup, celery soup, ⅓ cup (80 ml) water and some salt and pepper. Spoon into sprayed 9 x 13-inch (23 x 33 cm) baking dish.
2. Bake covered at 350° (176° C) for 40 minutes.
3. Remove from oven, uncover and sprinkle cheese over casserole. Bake another 5 minutes.

Ham or Beef Spread

2 cups ham or roast beef	500 ml
¾ cup sweet pickle relish	180 ml
2 celery ribs, finely chopped	2
2 hard-boiled eggs, chopped	2
½ onion, finely chopped, mayonnaise	½

1. Chop meat in food processor and add relish, celery, eggs and onion and a little salt and pepper.
2. Fold in enough mayonnaise to make mixture spreadable and chill.
3. Spread on crackers or bread for sandwiches.

Ham 'N Cheese Mashed Potatoes

2 cups instant mashed potatoes	500 ml
¾ teaspoon garlic powder	4 ml
2 cups diced, cooked ham	500 ml
1 (8 ounce) package shredded cheddar cheese	1 (228 g)
½ cup whipping cream	125 ml

1. In bowl, combine potatoes and garlic powder. Spread in buttered 2-quart (2 L) baking dish and sprinkle them with ham.
2. Fold cheese into whipping cream and spoon over ham.
3. Bake uncovered at 400° (204° C) for 15 minutes or until golden brown.

Ham-Broccoli Stromboli

1 (10 ounce) package refrigerated pizza dough	**1 (284 g)**
1 (10 ounce) package frozen chopped broccoli, drained	**1 (284 g)**
1 (10 ounce) can cream of celery soup	**1 (284 g)**
3 cups diced, cooked ham	**750 ml**
1 cup shredded cheddar cheese	**250 ml**

1. Unroll dough onto greased baking sheet and set aside. Cook broccoli according to package directions and drain.
2. Mix broccoli, soup and ham. Spread ham mixture down center of dough and top with cheese. Fold long sides of dough over filling, pinch and seal. Pinch short side to seal.
3. Bake uncovered at 400° (204° C) for 20 minutes or until golden brown. Slice and serve.

Hamwiches

1 (8 ounce) can refrigerated crescent rolls	**1 (228 g)**
2 tablespoons mayonnaise	**30 ml**
2 teaspoons prepared mustard	**10 ml**
1¼ cups finely chopped, cooked ham	**310 ml**
½ cup shredded Swiss cheese	**125 ml**

1. Unroll dough and separate into 4 rectangles. Press seams to seal.
2. Combine mayonnaise and mustard and spread over rectangles, leaving ½-inch (1 cm) border. Sprinkle ham and cheese evenly over half of each rectangle and moisten edges with water. Fold dough over and pinch edges to seal.
3. Bake at 375° (190° C) for 10 to 15 minutes or until puffed and golden.

SWEETS

Favorite Cake

1 (18 ounce) butter pecan cake mix	1 (520 g)
1 cup bits o'brickle almond-toffee bits	250 ml
1 cup chopped pecans	250 ml
Powdered sugar	

1. Prepare cake mix according to package directions. Fold in almond-toffee bits and pecans.
2. Pour into greased, floured bundt cake pan. Bake at 350° (176° C) for 45 minutes or until toothpick inserted in center comes out clean.
3. Allow cake to cool several minutes and then remove cake from pan. Dust with sifted powdered sugar.

Cherry-Pineapple Cake

1 (20 ounce) can crushed pineapple, drained	1 (570 g)
1 (20 ounce) can cherry pie filling	1 (570 g)
1 (18 ounce) yellow cake mix	1 (520 g)
1 cup (2 sticks) butter, softened	250 ml
1¼ cups chopped pecans	310 ml

1. Place all ingredients in mixing bowl and mix by hand.
2. Pour into greased, floured 9 x 13-inch (23 x 33 cm) baking dish.
3. Bake at 350° (176° C) for 1 hour 10 minutes.

Easy Pineapple Cake

2 cups sugar	500 ml
2 cups flour	500 ml
1 (20 ounce) can crushed pineapple with juice	1 (570 g)
1 teaspoon baking soda	5 ml
1 teaspoon vanilla	5 ml

1. Mix by hand and combine all cake ingredients. Pour into greased, floured 9 x 13-inch (23 x 33 cm) baking pan.
2. Bake at 350° (176° C) for 30 to 35 minutes.

Don't worry–this is right–there are <u>no</u> eggs in this recipe!

Easy Pineapple Cake Icing:

1 (8 ounce) package cream cheese, softened	1 (228 g)
½ cup (1 stick) butter, melted	125 ml
1 cup powdered sugar	250 ml
1 cup chopped pecans	250 ml

1. Beat cream cheese, butter and powdered sugar with mixer. Add chopped pecans and pour over HOT cake.

Strawberry-Pound Cake

1 (18 ounce) box strawberry cake mix	1 (520 g)
1 (3½ ounce) package instant pineapple	
pudding mix or coconut cream	1 (100 g)
⅓ cup oil	80 ml
4 eggs	4
1 (3 ounce) package strawberry gelatin	1 (85 g)

1. Mix all ingredients plus 1 cup (250 ml) water and beat for 2 minutes at medium speed. Pour into greased, floured bundt pan.
2. Bake at 325° (163° C) for 55 to 60 minutes. Cake is done when toothpick comes out clean.
3. Cool for 20 minutes before removing cake from pan. If you would like an icing, use a commercial vanilla icing.

Two-Surprise Cake

1 bakery orange-chiffon cake	1
1 (15 ounce) can crushed pineapple with juice	1 (438 g)
1 (3.4 ounce) package vanilla instant pudding	1 (100 g)
1 (8 ounce) carton whipped topping	1 (228 g)
½ cup slivered almonds, toasted	125 ml

1. Slice cake horizontally to make 3 layers.
2. Mix pineapple, pudding and whipped topping and blend well.
3. Spread on each layer and cover top of cake. Sprinkle almonds on top and chill.

The first surprise is how easy it is and the second surprise is how good it is! You'll make this more than once.

Chocolate-Orange Cake

1 (16 ounce) loaf frozen pound cake, thawed	1 (454 g)
1 (12 ounce) jar orange marmalade	1 (340 g)
1 (16 ounce) can ready-to-spread chocolate-fudge frosting	1 (454 g)

1. Cut cake horizontally into 3 layers. Place one layer on cake platter. Spread with half marmalade. Place second layer over first and spread on remaining marmalade.
2. Top with third cake layer and spread frosting liberally on top and sides of cake and chill.

Poppy Seed Bundt Cake

1 (18 ounce) package yellow cake mix	1 (520 g)
1 (3.4 ounce) package instant coconut cream pudding mix	1 (96 g)
½ cup oil	125 ml
3 eggs	3
2 tablespoons poppy seeds	30 ml

1. In mixing bowl, combine cake mix and pudding mix, 1 cup (250 ml) water, oil and eggs. Beat on low speed until moist. Beat on medium speed for 2 minutes.
2. Stir in poppy seeds. Pour into greased, floured bundt pan.
3. Bake at 350° (176° C) for 50 minutes or until toothpick inserted near center comes out clean. Cool for 10 minutes and remove from pan. Dust with powdered sugar.

Blueberry Pound Cake

1 (18 ounce) box yellow cake mix	1 (520 g)
1 (8 ounce) package cream cheese, softened	1 (228 g)
½ cup oil	125 ml
4 eggs	4
1 (15 ounce) can whole blueberries, drained	1 (438 g)

1. With mixer, combine all ingredients and beat for 3 minutes. Pour into greased, floured bundt or tube pan.
2. Bake at 350° (176° C) for 50 minutes. Test with toothpick to be sure cake is done.
3. Sprinkle powdered sugar over top of cake.

Cherry Cake

1 (18 ounce) box French vanilla cake mix	1 (438 g)
½ cup (1 stick) butter, melted	125 ml)
2 eggs	2
1 (20 ounce) can cherry pie filling	1 (570 g)
1 cup chopped pecans	250 ml

1. In large bowl, mix all ingredients.
2. Pour into greased, floured bundt or tube pan.
3. Bake at 350° (176° C) for 1 hour. Sprinkle powdered sugar on top of cake, if you like.

Chocolate-Cherry Cake

1 (18 ounce) milk chocolate cake mix	1 (520 g)
1 (20 ounce) can cherry pie filling	1 (570 g)
3 eggs	3

1. In mixing bowl, combine cake mix, pie filling and eggs. Mix by hand. Pour into greased, floured 9 x 13-inch (23 x 33 cm) baking dish.
2. Bake at 350° (176° C) for 35 to 40 minutes. Test with toothpick for doneness.
3. Spread Chocolate-Cherry Cake Frosting over hot cake.

Chocolate-Cherry Cake Frosting:

5 tablespoons butter	75 ml
1¼ cups sugar	310 ml
½ cup milk	125 ml
1 (6 ounce) package chocolate chips	1 (170 g)

1. When cake is done, combine butter, sugar and milk in a medium saucepan. Boil 1 minute, stirring constantly.   Add chocolate chips and stir until chips melt. Pour over hot cake.

This is a chocolate lover's dream.

Hawaiian-Dream Cake

1 (18 ounce) yellow cake mix	1 (520 g)
4 eggs	4
¾ cup oil	180 ml
½ (20 ounce) can crushed pineapple with	
½ juice	1 (570 g)

1. With mixer beat all ingredients for 4 minutes.
2. Pour into greased, floured 9 x 13-inch (23 x 33 cm) baking pan.
3. Bake at 350° (176° C) for 30 to 35 minutes or until cake tests done with toothpick. Cool and spread Coconut Pineapple Icing over cake.

Coconut-Pineapple Icing:

½ (20 ounce) can crushed pineapple with juice	1 (570 g)
½ cup (1 stick) butter	125 ml
1 (16 ounce) box powdered sugar	1 (454 g)
1 (6 ounce) can flaked coconut	1 (170 g)

1. Heat pineapple and butter and boil 2 minutes. Add powdered sugar and coconut. Punch holes in cake with knife. Pour hot icing over cake.

*This looks like a lot of trouble to make, but it
really isn't – and it is a wonderful cake!*

Old-Fashion Applesauce Spice Cake

1 (18 ounce) box spice cake mix	**1 (520 g)**
3 eggs	**3**
1¼ cups applesauce	**310 ml**
⅓ cup oil	**80 ml**
1 cup chopped pecans	**250 ml**

1. With mixer, combine cake mix, eggs, applesauce and oil. Beat at medium speed for 2 minutes. Stir in pecans.
2. Pour into 9 x 13-inch (23 x 33 cm) greased, floured baking pan. Bake at 350° (176° C) for 40 minutes. Test until toothpick comes out clean. Cool.
3. For frosting, use prepared vanilla frosting and add ½ teaspoon (2 ml) cinnamon.

This cake would also be good with Coconut-Pineapple Icing on page 250.

Coconut Cake Deluxe

1 (18 ounce) package yellow cake mix (plus ingredients called for in cake mix)	1 (520 g)
1 (14 ounce) can sweetened condensed milk	1 (420 g)
1 (15 ounce) can coconut cream	1 (438 g)
½ cup flaked coconut	125 ml
1 (8 ounce) carton whipped topping	1 (228 g)

1. Mix yellow cake according to directions with ingredients called for. Pour into greased, floured 9 x 13-inch (23 x 33 cm) baking pan. Bake in at 350° (176° C) for 30 to 35 minutes or until toothpick inserted in center comes out clean.
2. While cake is warm, punch holes in cake about 2 inches (5 cm) apart. Pour sweetened condensed milk over cake and spread around until all milk soaks into cake. Pour coconut cream over cake and sprinkle flaked coconut on top.
3. Cool, frost with whipped topping and chill.

This is a fabulous cake!

Gooey Butter Cake

1 (18 ounce) box butter cake mix	1 (520 g)
½ cup (1 stick) butter, melted	125 ml
4 eggs, divided	4
1 (16 ounce) box powdered sugar	1 (454 g)
1 (8 ounce) package cream cheese, softened	1 (228 g)

1. With mixer, beat 2 eggs with cake mix and butter. Spread mixture into greased, floured 9 x 13-inch (23 x 33 cm) baking pan.
2. Reserve ¾ cup (180 ml) powdered sugar for topping. Mix remaining powdered sugar, 2 remaining eggs and cream cheese and beat until smooth. Spread mixture on top of dough. Sprinkle remaining sugar on top.
3. Bake cake at 350° (176° C) for 40 minutes. Cake will puff up and then go down when it cools.

Angel-Cream Cake

1 large angel food cake	1
1 (18 ounce) jar chocolate ice cream topping	1 (520 g)
½ gallon vanilla ice cream, softened	2 L
1 (12 ounce) carton whipped topping	1 (340 g)
½ cup slivered almonds, toasted	125 ml

1. Tear cake into large pieces. Stir in chocolate topping to coat pieces of cake and mix in softened ice cream. Work fast! Stir into tube pan and freeze overnight.
2. Turn out onto large cake plate and frost with whipped topping. Decorate with almonds and freeze.

Strawberry-Angel Delight Cake

1 cup sweetened condensed milk	250 ml
¼ cup lemon juice	60 ml
1 pint fresh strawberries, halved	500 ml
1 angel food cake	1
1 pint heavy cream, whipped	500 ml

1. Combine condensed milk and lemon juice. Fold in strawberries.
2. Slice cake in half horizontally. Spread strawberry filling on bottom layer. Place top layer over filling.
3. Cover with whipped cream and top with extra strawberries.

Golden Rum Cake

1 (18 ounce) box yellow cake mix with pudding	1 (520 g)
3 eggs	3
⅓ cup oil	80 ml
½ cup rum	125 ml
1 cup chopped pecans	250 ml

1. Blend cake mix, eggs, 1⅓ cups (330 ml) water, oil and rum with mixer.
2. Stir in pecans. Pour into greased, floured 10-inch tube or bundt pan.
3. Bake at 325° (163° C) for 1 hour. (You might want to sprinkle powdered sugar over cooled cake.)

Chess Cake

1 (18 ounce) box yellow cake mix	**1 (520 g)**
2 eggs	**2**
½ cup (1 stick) butter, softened	**125 ml**
Topping: 2 eggs	**2**
1 (8 ounce) package cream cheese, softened	**1 (228 g)**
1 (1 pound) box powdered sugar	**1 (454 g)**

1. Beat cake mix, 2 eggs and butter. Press into greased 9 x 13-inch (23 x 33 cm) baking pan.
2. Beat 2 eggs, cream cheese and powdered sugar and pour over cake.
3. Bake at 350° (176° C) for 35 minutes.

Pound Cake

1 cup (2 sticks) butter, softened	**250 ml**
2 cups sugar	**500 ml**
5 eggs	**5**
2 cups flour	**500 ml**
1 tablespoon almond flavoring	**15 ml**

1. Combine all ingredients in mixing bowl and beat for 10 minutes at medium speed.
2. Pour into greased, floured tube pan. (Batter will be very thick.)
3. Bake at 325° (163° C) for 1 hour. Test with toothpick for doneness.

Pound Cake Deluxe

1 bakery pound cake	**1**
1 (15 ounce) can crushed pineapple with juice	**1 (438 g)**
1 (3.4 ounce) package coconut instant pudding mix	**1 (100 g)**
1 (8 ounce) carton whipped topping	**1 (228 g)**
½ cup flaked coconut	**125 ml**

1. Slice cake horizontally and make 3 layers.
2. Mix pineapple, pudding and whipped topping together and blend well.
3. Spread on each layer, sprinkle top of cake with coconut and chill.

Pineapple-Angel Cake

1 (1-step) angel food cake mix	**1**
1 (20 ounce) can crushed pineapple with juice	**1 (570 g)**

1. Place angel food cake mix in mixing bowl and pour pineapple. Beat according to directions on cake mix box.
2. Pour into ungreased 9 x 13-inch (23 x 33 cm) baking pan.
3. Bake at 350° (176° C) for 30 minutes. (This is a good low calorie cake, but if you want it iced, use a prepared vanilla icing.)

Quick Fruitcake

1 (15.6 ounce) package cranberry or	
blueberry quick-bread mix	1 (435 g)
½ cup chopped pecans	125 ml
½ cup chopped dates	125 ml
¼ cup chopped maraschino cherries	60 ml
¼ cup crushed pineapple, drained	60 ml

1. Prepare quick-bread batter according to package directions. Stir in remaining ingredients. Pour into 9 x 5-inch (23 x 13 cm) greased loaf pan.
2. Bake at 350° (176° C) for 60 minutes or until a toothpick inserted in cake comes out clean. Cool 10 minutes before removing from pan.

Easy Cheesecake

2 (8 ounce) packages cream cheese, softened	2 (228 g)
½ cup sugar	125 ml
½ teaspoon vanilla	2 ml
2 eggs	2
1 (9 inch) graham cracker piecrust	1 (240 g)

1. In mixing bowl, beat cream cheese, sugar, vanilla and eggs.
2. Pour into piecrust.
3. Bake at 350° (176° C) for 40 minutes. Cool and serve with any pie filling.

Cranberry Coffee Cake

2 eggs	**2**
1 cup mayonnaise	**250 ml**
1 (18 ounce) box spice cake mix	**1 (520 g)**
1 (16 ounce) can whole cranberry sauce	**1 (454 g)**
Powdered sugar	

1. With mixing bowl, beat eggs, mayonnaise and cake mix and mix well. Fold in cranberry sauce.
2. Pour into greased, floured 9 x 13-inch (23 x 33 cm) baking pan.
3. Bake at 325° (163° C) for 45 minutes. Test with toothpick to be sure cake is done. When cake is cool, dust with powdered sugar. (If you would rather have icing than powdered sugar, use prepared icing.)

Sunny Lime Pie

2 (6 ounce) cartons key lime pie yogurt	2 (170 g)
1 (3 ounce) package dry lime gelatin	1 (85 g)
1 (8 ounce) carton whipped topping	1 (228 g)
1 (9 inch) graham cracker piecrust	1 (240 g)

1. In a bowl, combine yogurt and lime gelatin and mix well.
2. Fold in whipped topping and spread in piecrust.
3. Freeze. Take out of freezer 20 minutes before slicing.

Nothing could be easier!

Creamy Lemon Pie

1 (8 ounce) package cream cheese, softened	1 (228 g)
1 (14 ounce) can sweetened condensed milk	1 (420 g)
¼ cup lemon juice	60 ml
1 (20 ounce) can lemon pie filling	1 (570 g)
1 (9 inch) graham cracker piecrust	1 (240 g)

1. In mixing bowl, beat cream cheese until creamy. Add sweetened condensed milk and lemon juice. Beat until mixture is very creamy.
2. Fold in lemon pie filling and stir until creamy.
3. Pour into piecrust. Refrigerate several hours before slicing and serving.

Cherry-Pecan Pie

1 (14 ounce) can sweetened condensed milk	1 (420 g)
¼ cup lemon juice	60 ml
1 (8 ounce) carton whipped topping	1 (228 g)
1 cup chopped pecans	250 ml
1 (20 ounce) can cherry pie filling	1 (570 g)

1. Combine condensed milk and lemon juice and stir well. Fold in whipped topping.
2. Fold pecans and pie filling into mixture.
3. Spoon into 2 graham cracker crusts. Chill overnight.

Chocolate-Cream Cheese Pie

1 (8 ounce) package cream cheese, softened	1 (228 g)
¾ cup powdered sugar	180 ml
¼ cup cocoa	60 ml
1 (8 ounce) container whipped topping, thawed	1 (228 g)
½ cup chopped pecans	125 ml

1. Combine cream cheese, sugar and cocoa in mixing bowl and beat at medium speed until creamy.
2. Add whipped topping and fold until smooth.
3. Spread in prepared crumb piecrust and sprinkle pecans over top. Refrigerate.

Coffee-Mallow Pie

1 tablespoon instant coffee granules	15 ml
4 cups miniature marshmallows	1 L
1 tablespoon butter	15 ml
1 (8 ounce) carton whipping cream, whipped	1 (228 g)
½ cup chopped walnuts, toasted	125 ml

1. In heavy saucepan, bring 1 cup (250 ml) water to a boil and stir in coffee until it dissolves. Reduce heat and add marshmallows and butter. Cook and stir over low heat until marshmallows melt and mixture is smooth.
2. Set saucepan in ice and whisk mixture constantly until it cools. Fold in whipped cream and spoon into 9-inch (23 cm) graham cracker piecrust.
3. Sprinkle with walnuts. Refrigerate for at least 4 hours before serving.

Cheese-Cake Pie

2 (8 ounce) packages cream cheese	2 (228 g)
3 eggs	3
¾ cup plus 4 tablespoons sugar	180 ml
1½ teaspoons vanilla	7 ml
1 (8 ounce) carton sour cream	1 (228 g)

1. In mixing bowl, combine cream cheese, eggs, ¾ cup (180 ml) sugar and ½ teaspoon (2 ml) vanilla and beat for 5 minutes.
2. Pour into sprayed 9-inch (23 cm) pie pan and bake at 350° (176° C) for 25 minutes. Cool for 20 minutes.
3. Combine sour cream, 4 tablespoons (60 ml) sugar and 1 teaspoon (5 ml) vanilla. Pour over cooled cake. Bake 10 minutes longer. Chill at least 4 hours. Serve with your favorite fruit topping.

Peach-Mousse Pie

1 (16 ounce) package frozen peach slices, thawed	1 (454 g)
1 cup sugar	250 ml
1 (1 ounce) envelope unflavored gelatin	1 (28 g)
⅛ teaspoon ground nutmeg	.5 ml
¾ (8 ounce) carton whipped topping	¾ (228 g)

1. Place peaches in blender and process until smooth. Place in saucepan, bring to boiling point and stir constantly. Combine sugar, gelatin and nutmeg. Stir into hot puree until sugar and gelatin dissolves.
2. Pour gelatin-peach mixture into large mixing bowl. Place in deep freeze until mixture mounds (about 20 minutes) and stir occasionally .
3. Beat mixture at high speed about 5 minutes until mixture becomes light and frothy. Fold in whipped topping and spoon into 9-inch (23 cm) graham cracker piecrust.

Incredibly good!

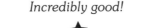

Creamy Pecan Pie

1½ cups light corn syrup	375 ml
1 (3 ounce) package vanilla instant pudding	1 (85 g)
3 eggs	3
3 tablespoons (⅓ stick) butter, melted	45 ml
2 cups pecan halves	500 ml

1. Combine corn syrup, pudding, eggs and butter, mix well and stir in pecans.
2. Pour into unbaked deep-dish pie shell. Cover piecrust edges with strips of foil to prevent excessive browning.
3. Bake at 325° (163° C) for 35 to 40 minutes or until center of pie sets.

Dixie Pie

24 large marshmallows	24
1 cup evaporated milk	250 ml
1 (8 ounce) carton whipping cream, whipped	1 (228 g)
3 tablespoons bourbon	45 ml
1 (9 inch) prepared chocolate piecrust	1 (23 cm)

1. In saucepan on low heat, melt marshmallows in milk and stir constantly. Do not boil. Cool in refrigerator. Fold into whipped cream while adding bourbon.
2. Pour into chocolate crust. Refrigerate at least 5 hours before serving.

Black Forest Pie

1½ cups whipping cream, whipped	375 ml
4 (1 ounce) bars unsweetened baking chocolate	4 (28 g)
1 (14 ounce) can sweetened condensed milk	1 (420 g)
1 teaspoon almond extract	5 ml
1 (20 ounce) can cherry pie filling, chilled	1 (570 g)

1. In saucepan, over medium low heat, melt chocolate with sweetened condensed milk and stir well to mix. Remove from heat and stir in extract. This mixture needs to cool.
2. With mixer, whip cream. When mixture is about room temperature, pour chocolate into whipped cream and fold gently until both combine.
3. Pour into prepared, cooked 9-inch (23 cm) piecrust. To serve, spoon a heaping spoonful of cherry pie filling over each piece of pie.

Definitely a party dessert, but the family will insist
it should be served on a regular basis.

Chess Pie

½ cup (1 stick) butter, softened	125 ml
2 cups sugar	500 ml
1 tablespoon cornstarch	15 ml
4 eggs	4
1 (9 inch) unbaked piecrust	1 (23 cm)

1. Cream butter, sugar and cornstarch. Add eggs, one at a time and beat well after each addition.
2. Pour mixture in piecrust. Cover piecrust edges with strips of foil to prevent excessive browning.
3. Bake at 325° (163° C) for 45 minutes or until center sets.

Merry-Berry Pie

1 (6 ounce) package strawberry gelatin	1 (170 g)
1 cup whole berry cranberry sauce	250 ml
½ cup cranberry juice cocktail	125 ml
1 (8 ounce) carton whipped topping	1 (228 g)
1 (9-inch) baked pie shell	1 (23 g)

1. Dissolve gelatin in 1 cup (250 ml) boiling water. Add cranberry sauce and juice. Chill until it begins to thicken.
2. Fold in whipped topping and chill again until mixture mounds. Pour into pie shell.
3. Refrigerate several hours before serving.

Peanut Butter Pie

⅔ cup crunchy peanut butter	160 ml
1 (8 ounce) package cream cheese, softened	1 (228 g)
½ cup milk	125 ml
1 cup powdered sugar	250 ml
1 (8 ounce) carton whipped topping	1 (228 g)

1. With mixer, blend peanut butter, cream cheese, milk and sugar and fold in whipped topping.
2. Pour into graham cracker crust. Refrigerate several hour before serving.

Pineapple-Cheese Pie

1 (14 ounce) can sweetened condensed milk	1 (420 g)
¼ cup lemon juice	60 ml
1 (8 ounce) package cream cheese, softened	1 (228 g)
1 (15 ounce) can crushed pineapple, well drained	1 (520 g)
1 (9-inch) graham cracker piecrust	1 (23 cm)

1. In mixing bowl, combine condensed milk, lemon juice and cream cheese. Beat slowly at first, then beat until smooth.
2. Fold in well drained pineapple and mix well.
3. Pour into prepared graham cracker crust. Chill 8 hours before slicing.

Pineapple-Lemon Pie

1 (14 ounce) can sweetened condensed milk	1 (420 g)
1 (20 ounce) can lemon pie filling	1 (570 g)
1 (20 ounce) can crushed pineapple, well drained	1 (570 g)
1 (8 ounce) carton whipped topping	1 (228 g)
2 (9 inch) cookie-flavored piecrusts	2 (23 cm)

1. With mixer, combine condensed milk and lemon pie filling and beat until smooth.
2. Add pineapple and whipped topping and gently fold into pie filling mixture.
3. Pour into 2 piecrusts and refrigerate. (Eat 1 and freeze other!)

Pineapple-Fluff Pie

1 (20 ounce) can crushed pineapple with juice	1 (570 g)
1 (3.4 ounce) package instant lemon pudding	1 (100 g)
1 (8 ounce) carton whipped topping	1 (228 g)
1 (9 inch) graham cracker crust	1 (23 cm)

1. In bowl, combine pineapple and pudding mix and beat until thick. Fold in whipped topping.
2. Spoon into piecrust. Refrigerate several hours before serving.

This pie is light, airy and full of fluff. It's a perfect dessert when you want a cool, summer finale.

Strawberry-Cream Cheese Pie

2 (10 ounce) packages frozen sweetened strawberries, thawed	2 (284 g)
2 (8 ounce) packages cream cheese, softened	2 (228 g)
1 cup powdered sugar	250 ml
1 (8 ounce) carton whipped topping	1 (228 g)
1 (9 inch) prepared chocolate crumb crust	1 (23 cm)

1. Drain strawberries and reserve ¼ cup (60 ml) liquid. In mixing bowl, combine cream cheese, reserved liquid, strawberries and sugar and beat well.
2. Fold in whipped topping and spoon into crust. Refrigerate overnight. Garnish with fresh strawberries.

Tumbleweed Pie

½ gallon vanilla ice cream, softened	2 L
⅓ cup plus 1 tablespoon kahlua	80 ml
⅓ cup plus 1 tablespoon amaretto	80 ml
1 (9 inch) prepared chocolate cookie crust	1 (23 cm)
¼ cup slivered almonds, toasted	60 ml

1. Place ice cream, kahlua and amaretto in mixing bowl and blend as quickly as possible. Pour into piecrust.
2. Sprinkle almonds over top and freeze.

Yum-Yum Strawberry Pie

2 pints fresh strawberries, divided	1 L
1¼ cups sugar	310 ml
3 tablespoons cornstarch	45 ml
1 (9 inch) graham cracker piecrust	1 (23 cm)
1 (8 ounce) carton whipping cream, whipped	1 (228 g)

1. Crush 1 pint (500 ml) strawberries; add sugar, cornstarch and a dash of salt. Cook on low heat until thick and clear. Cool.
2. Place other pint strawberries in pie shell. Cover with cooked mixture.
3. Top with whipping cream and refrigerate.

Grasshopper Pie

22 large marshmallows	22
⅓ cup creme de menthe	80 ml
2 (8 ounce) cartons whipping cream, whipped	2 (228 g)
1 (9 inch) prepared chocolate piecrust	1 (23 cm)

1. In large saucepan, melt marshmallows with creme de menthe over low heat.
2. Cool and fold whipped cream into marshmallow mixture.
3. Pour filling into piecrust and freeze until ready to serve.

Lemonade Pie

1 (9 inch) graham cracker piecrust	**1 (23 cm)**
½ gallon vanilla ice cream, softened	**2 L**
1 (6 ounce) can frozen lemonade concentrate	**1 (170 g)**

1. With mixer, combine ice cream and frozen lemonade. Work quickly.
2. Pile ice cream mixture in piecrust and freeze.

Pink Lemonade Pie

1 (6 ounce) can frozen pink lemonade concentrate, thawed	**1 (170 g)**
1 (14 ounce) can sweetened condensed milk	**1 (420 g)**
1 (12 ounce) carton whipped topping	**1 (340 g)**
1 (9 inch) graham cracker piecrust	**1 (23 cm)**

1. In large bowl, combine lemonade concentrate and condensed milk and mix well.
2. Fold in whipped topping.
3. Pour into piecrust. Refrigerate several hours.

Sweet Potato Pie

1 (14 ounce) can sweet potatoes	1 (420 g)
¾ cup milk	180 ml
1 cup firmly packed brown sugar	250 ml
2 eggs	2
½ teaspoon ground cinnamon	2 ml

1. Combine all ingredients plus ½ teaspoon (2 ml) salt in mixing bowl and blend until smooth.
2. Pour into 9-inch (23 cm) unbaked piecrust.
3. Bake at 350° (176° C) for 40 minutes or until knife inserted in center comes out clean. (Shield edges of pastry with aluminum foil to prevent excessive browning.)

Easy Pumpkin Pie

1 (9-inch) unbaked deep-dish pie shell	1 (23 cm)
2 eggs	2
3¼ cups (30 ounce can) pumpkin pie mix	810 ml
⅔ cup evaporated milk	160 ml

1. Beat eggs lightly in large bowl. Stir in pumpkin pie mix and evaporated milk. Pour into pie shell. Cut 2-inch (5 cm) wide strips of foil and cover piecrust edges. This will keep piecrust from getting too brown.
2. Bake at 400° (204° C) for 15 minutes. Reduce temperature to 350° (176° C) and bake for 50 more minutes or until knife inserted in center come out clean.
3. Cool.

Apricot Cobbler

1 (20 ounce) can apricot pie filling	1 (570 g)
1 (20 ounce) can crushed pineapple with juice	1 (570 g)
1 cup chopped pecans	250 ml
1 (18 ounce) yellow cake mix	1 (520 g)
1 cup (2 sticks) butter, melted	250 ml

1. Spray 9 x 13-inch (23 x 33 cm) baking dish. Pour pie filling in pan and spread out.
2. Spoon pineapple and juice over pie filling. Sprinkle pecans over pineapple. Sprinkle cake mix over pecans. Drizzle melted butter over cake mix.
3. Bake at 375° (190° C) for 40 minutes or until light brown and crunchy. It's great topped with whipped topping. Serve hot or room temperature.

So easy and so good!

Cherry-Strawberry Cobbler

1 (20 ounce) can strawberry pie filling	1 (570 g)
1 (20 ounce) can cherry pie filling	1 (570 g)
1 (18 ounce) package white cake mix	1 (520 g)
1 cup (2 sticks) butter, melted	250 ml
¾ cup package slivered almonds	180 ml

1. Spread pie fillings in greased 9 x 13-inch (23 x 33 cm) sprayed baking pan. Sprinkle cake mix over pie fillings.
2. Drizzle melted butter over top. Sprinkle almonds over top.
3. Bake at 350° (176° C) for 55 minutes. Top with whipped topping.

Peach Crisp

4¾ cups peeled, sliced peaches	1 L
	180 ml
3 tablespoons lemon juice	45 ml
1 cup flour	250 ml
1¾ cups sugar	430 ml
1 egg, beaten	1

1. Place peaches in 9-inch (23 cm) baking dish and sprinkle lemon juice over top.
2. Mix flour, sugar, egg and dash of salt. Spread mixture over top of peaches. Dot with a little butter.
3. Bake at 375° (190° C) until golden brown.

Cherry-Cinnamon Cobbler

1 (20 ounce) can cherry pie filling	1 (570 g)
1 (12.4 ounce) tube refrigerated cinnamon rolls	1 (354 g)

1. Spread pie filling into a greased 8-inch (20 cm) baking dish. Set aside icing from cinnamon rolls. Arrange rolls around edge of baking dish.
2. Bake at 400° (204° C) for 15 minutes. Cover and bake 10 minutes longer. Spread icing over rolls and serve warm.

Blueberry Crunch

1 (20 ounce) can crushed pineapple with juice	1 (570 g)
1 (18 ounce) package yellow cake mix	1 (520 g)
3 cups fresh or frozen blueberries	750 ml
⅔ cup sugar	160 ml
½ cup (1 stick) butter, melted	125 ml

1. Spread pineapple in buttered 9 x 13-inch (23 x 33 cm) baking dish. Sprinkle with cake mix, blueberries and sugar. Drizzle with butter. (It is even better if you add 1 cup (250 ml) chopped pecans.)
2. Bake at 350° (176° C) for 45 minutes or until bubbly.

Blueberry Cobbler

½ cup (1 stick) butter, melted	125 ml
1 cup self-rising flour	250 ml
1¾ cups sugar	430 ml
1 cup milk	250 ml
1 (20 ounce) can blueberry pie filling	1 (570 g)

1. Pour butter in a 9-inch (23 cm) baking pan. Mix flour and sugar in bowl, slowly add milk and stir. Pour over melted butter, but do not stir.
2. Spoon pie filling over batter and bake at 300° (149° C) for 1 hour.
3. To serve, top with whipped topping.

Vanishing Butter Cookies

1 (18 ounce) box butter cake mix	1 (520 g)
1 (3 ounce) package butterscotch instant pudding mix	1 (85 g)
1 cup oil	250 ml
1 egg, beaten	1
1¼ cups chopped pecans	310 ml

1. Mix by hand (not with mixer), cake mix and pudding mix. Stir in oil.
2. Add egg and mix thoroughly. Stir in pecans. With a teaspoon or small cookie scoop, place cookie dough on cookie sheet about 2 inches (5 cm) apart.
3. Bake at 350° (176° C) for 8 or 9 minutes. Do not overcook.

Lemon Drops

½ (8 ounce) carton whipped topping	½ (228 g)
1 (18 ounce) box lemon cake mix	1 (520 g)
1 egg	1
Powdered sugar	

1. Stir, by hand, whipped topping into lemon cake mix. Add egg and mix thoroughly.
2. Shape into balls and roll in powdered sugar
3. Bake at 350° (176° C) for 8 to 10 minutes. Do not overcook.

Chocolate Macaroons

1 (4 ounce) package sweet baking chocolate	1 (115 g)
2 egg whites, room temperature	2
½ cup sugar	125 ml
¼ teaspoon vanilla	1 ml
1 (7 ounce) can flaked coconut	1 (198 g)

1. Place chocolate in top of double boiler. Cook until chocolate melts, stirring occasionally. Remove from heat and cool.
2. Beat egg whites at high speed for 1 minute. Gradually add sugar, 1 tablespoon (15 ml) at a time, and beat until stiff peaks form (about 3 minutes). Add chocolate and vanilla and beat well. Stir in coconut.
3. Drop by teaspoonfuls onto cookie sheet lined with brown paper. Bake at 350° (176° C) for 12 to 15 minutes. Transfer cookies from brown paper to cooling rack. Carefully remove cookies from brown paper.

Chocolate Chip Cheese Bars

1 (18 ounce) tube refrigerated chocolate chip cookie dough	1 (520 g)
1 (8 ounce) package cream cheese, softened	1 (228 g)
½ cup sugar	125 ml
1 egg	1

1. Cut cookie dough in half. For crust, press half dough onto bottom of greased 9-inch (23 cm) square baking pan or 7 x 11-inch (18 x 28 cm) baking pan.
2. In mixing bowl, beat cream cheese, sugar and egg until smooth. Spread over crust and crumble remaining dough over top.
3. Bake at 350° (176° C) for 35 to 40 minutes or until toothpick inserted near center comes out clean. Cool on wire rack. Cut into bars and refrigerate leftovers.

Coconut Nibbles

2 cups flakey wheat cereal	500 ml
1¼ cups shredded coconut	310 ml
2 large egg whites	2
1¼ cups sugar	310 ml
½ teaspoon vanilla	2 ml

1. Preheat oven to 350° (176° C). Prepare baking sheet with non-stick spray.
2. Combine cereal and coconut in large bowl and mix well. Beat egg whites with mixer at high speed until soft peaks form. Gradually add sugar and vanilla while mixing.
3. Fold egg whites into cereal-coconut mixture and mix well. Drop by tablespoonfuls about 2 inches (5 cm) apart and bake about 8 to 10 minutes. Watch closely and remove Coconut Nibbles from oven when they become golden brown. Do not let them get too brown on bottom. Store in airtight container.

Chocolate Kisses

2 egg whites, room temperature	2
⅔ cup sugar	160 ml
1 teaspoon vanilla	5 ml
1¼ cups chopped pecans	310 ml
1 (6 ounce) package chocolate chips	1 (170 g)

1. Preheat oven to 375° (190° C). Beat egg whites until very stiff. Blend in sugar, vanilla and dash of salt. Fold in pecans and chocolate chips.
2. Drop on shiny side of foil on cookie sheet.
3. Put cookies in oven; TURN OVEN OFF and leave overnight. If a little sticky, leave out in air to dry.

Chocolate Drops

1 (6 ounce) package milk chocolate chips	**1 (170 g)**
⅔ cup chunky peanut butter	**160 ml**
4¼ cups cocoa krispie cereal	**1 L 60 ml**

1. In double boiler, melt chocolate chips and stir in peanut butter.
2. Stir in cereal. Press into 9 x 9-inch (23 x 23 cm) pan and cut into bars.

Chocolate-Crunch Cookies

1 (18 ounce) package German chocolate cake mix with pudding	**1 (520 g)**
1 egg, slightly beaten	**1**
½ cup (1 stick) butter, melted	**125 ml**
1 cup crisp rice cereal	**250 ml**

1. Combine cake mix, egg and butter. Add cereal and stir until blended. Shape dough into 1-inch (2.5 cm) balls. Place on lightly greased cookie sheet.
2. Dip a fork in flour and flatten cookies in crisscross pattern.
3. Bake at 350° (176° C) for 10 to 12 minutes and cool.

These cookies are not only incredible easy, this recipe is wonderful for kids when they want to bake.

Chocolate-Coconut Cookies

1 cup sweetened condensed milk	250 ml
4 cups flaked coconut	1 L
⅔ cup miniature semi-sweet chocolate bits	160 ml
1 teaspoon vanilla	5 ml
½ teaspoon almond extract	2 ml

1. Combine milk and coconut. (Mixture will be gooey.) Add chocolate bits, vanilla and almond and stir until well blended.
2. Drop by teaspoonfuls onto sprayed cookie sheet. Bake at 325° (163° C) for 12 minutes.
3. Store in airtight container.

Peanut Butter-Date Cookies

1 egg, beaten	1
⅔ cup granulated sugar	160 ml
⅓ cup packed brown sugar	80 ml
1 cup chunky peanut butter	250 ml
½ cup chopped dates	125 ml

1. Blend egg, sugars and peanut butter and mix thoroughly. Stir in dates and roll into 1-inch (2.5 cm) balls.
2. Place on ungreased cookie sheet. Use fork to press ball down to about ½ inch (1 cm).
3. Bake at 350° (176° C) for about 12 minutes. Cool before storing.

Easy Peanut Butter Cookies

1 (18 ounce) package prepared sugar cookie dough	1 (520 g)
½ cup creamy peanut butter	125 ml
½ cup miniature chocolate chips	125 ml
½ cup peanut butter chips	125 ml
½ cup chopped peanuts	125 ml

1. Beat cookie dough and peanut butter in large bowl until blended and smooth.
2. Stir in remaining ingredients. Drop 1 heaping tablespoon (15 cm) dough onto ungreased baking sheet.
3. Bake at 350° (176° C) for 15 minutes. Cool on wire rack.

Chinese Cookies

1 (6 ounce) package butterscotch chips	1 (170 g)
1 (6 ounce) package milk chocolate chips	1 (170 g)
2 cups chow mein noodles	500 ml
1¼ cups salted peanuts	310 ml

1. On low heat, melt butterscotch and chocolate chips.
2. Pour over noodles and peanuts and mix well. Drop by teaspoon onto wax paper.
3. Refrigerate to harden. Store in airtight container.

Yummy Cookies

3 egg whites	3
1¼ cups sugar	310 ml
2 teaspoons vanilla	10 ml
3½ cups frosted flakes	675 ml
1 cup chopped pecans	250 ml

1. Beat egg whites until stiff. Gradually add sugar and vanilla.
2. Fold in frosted flakes and pecans. Drop by teaspoonfuls on cookie sheet lined with wax paper.
3. Bake at 250° (121° C) for 40 minutes.

Potato Chip Crispies

1 cup (2 sticks) butter, softened	250 ml
⅔ cups sugar	140 ml
1 teaspoon vanilla	5 ml
1½ cups flour	375 ml
½ cup crushed potato chips	125 ml

1. Cream butter, sugar and vanilla. Add flour and chips and mix well.
2. Drop by teaspoonfuls on ungreased cookie sheet.
3. Bake at 350° (176° C) for about 12 minutes or until light brown.

These are really good and crunchy!

Brown Sugar Wafers

1 cup (2 sticks) butter, softened	250 ml
¾ cup packed dark brown sugar	180 ml
1 egg yolk	1
1 tablespoon vanilla	15 ml
1¼ cups flour	310 ml

1. With mixer, beat butter and gradually add brown sugar. Add egg yolk and vanilla and beat well.
2. Add flour and dash salt and mix well. Shape dough into 1-inch (2.5 cm) balls and chill 2 hours.
3. Place on cookie sheet and flatten each cookie. Bake at 350° (176° C) for 10 to 12 minutes.

Angel Macaroons

1 (16 ounce) package 1-step angel food cake mix	1 (454 g)
½ cup water	125 ml
1½ teaspoons almond extract	7 ml
2 cups flaked coconut	500 ml

1. With mixer, beat cake mix, water and extract on low speed for 30 seconds. Scrape bowl and beat on medium for 1 minute. Fold in coconut.
2. Drop by rounded teaspoonfuls onto parchment paper-lined baking sheet.
3. Bake at 350° (176° C) for 10 to 12 minutes or until set. Remove paper with cookies to wire rack to cool.

Hello Dollies

1½ cups graham cracker crumbs	375 ml
1 (6 ounce) package chocolate chips	1 (170 g)
1 cup flaked coconut	250 ml
1¼ cups chopped pecans	310 ml
1 (14 ounce) can sweetened condensed milk	1 (420 g)

1. Sprinkle cracker crumbs in 9 x 9-inch (23 x 23 cm) pan. Layer chocolate chips, coconut and pecans. Pour condensed milk over top of layered ingredients.
2. Bake at 350° (176° C) for 25 to 30 minutes. Cool and cut into squares.

Marshmallow Treats

¼ cup (½ stick) butter	60 ml
4 cups miniature marshmallows	1 L
½ cup chunky peanut butter	125 ml
5 cups crispy rice cereal	1.25 L

1. In saucepan, melt butter and add marshmallows. Stir until they melt and add peanut butter. Remove from heat.
2. Add cereal and stir well.
3. Press mixture into 9 x 13-inch (23 x 33 cm) pan. Cut in squares when cool.

Praline Grahams

⅓ (16 ounce) box graham crackers	1 (454 g)
¾ cup (1½ sticks) butter	180 ml
½ cup sugar	125 ml
1 cup chopped pecans	250 ml

1. Separate each graham cracker into 4 sections. Arrange in jelly-roll pan with edges touching.
2. Melt butter in saucepan and stir in sugar and pecans. Bring to a boil and cook 3 minutes, stirring frequently.
3. Spread mixture evenly over graham crackers. Bake at 300° (149° C) for 10 to 12 minutes. Remove from pan and cool on wax paper. Break up to serve.

Coconut Yummies

1 (12 ounce) package white chocolate baking chips	1 (340 g)
¼ cup (½ stick) butter	60 ml
16 large marshmallows	16
2 cups quick-cooking oats	500 ml
1 cup flaked coconut	250 ml

1. In saucepan over low heat, melt chocolate chips, butter and marshmallows and stir until smooth.
2. Stir in oats and coconut and mix well.
3. Drop by rounded teaspoonfuls onto wax paper-lined baking sheets. Chill until set. Store in airtight container.

Sand Tarts

1 cup (2 sticks) butter, softened	**250 ml**
¾ cup powdered sugar	**180 ml**
2 cups sifted flour	**500 ml**
1 cup chopped pecans	**250 ml**
1 teaspoon vanilla	**5 ml**

1. In mixer, cream butter and sugar; add flour, pecans and vanilla.
2. Roll into crescents and place on ungreased cookie sheet.
3. Bake at 325° (163° C) for 20 minutes. Roll in extra powdered sugar after tarts cool.

Scotch Shortbread

1 cup butter	**250 ml**
2 cups flour	**500 ml**
¾ cup cornstarch	**180 ml**
⅔ cup sugar	**160 ml**
Granulated sugar	

1. Melt butter and stir in flour, cornstarch and sugar. Press into 9-inch (23 cm) square pan.
2. Bake at 325° (163° C) for 45 minutes. Cut into squares immediately after removing from oven. Sprinkle with colored-sugar sprinkles or granulated sugar.

Orange Balls

1 (12 ounce) box vanilla wafers, crushed	1 (340 g)
½ cup (1 stick) butter, melted	125 ml
1 (16 ounce) box powdered sugar	1 (454 g)
1 (6 ounce) can frozen orange juice concentrate	1 (170 g)
1 cup finely chopped pecans	250 ml

1. Combine wafers, butter, sugar and orange juice and mix well.
2. Form into balls and roll in chopped pecans. Store in airtight container.

You can also make these in finger shapes. These make neat cookies for a party or for a tea.

Rocky Road Bars

1 (12 ounce) package semi-sweet chocolate morsels	1 (340 g)
1 (14 ounce) can sweetened condensed milk	1 (420 g)
2 tablespoons (¼ stick) butter	30 ml
2 cups dry-roasted peanuts	500 ml
1 (10 ounce) package miniature marshmallows	1 (284 g)

1. Place chocolate morsels, milk and butter in top of double boiler. Heat until chocolate and butter melt, stirring constantly.
2. Remove from heat and stir in peanuts and marshmallows.
3. Spread mixture quickly on wax paper-lined 9 x 13-inch (23 x 33 cm) pan. Chill at least 2 hours. Cut into bars and store in refrigerator.

Nutty Blonde Brownies

1 (1 pound) box light brown sugar	1 (454 g)
4 eggs	4
2 cups biscuit mix	500 ml
2 cups chopped pecans	500 ml

1. In mixing bowl, beat brown sugar, eggs and biscuit mix.
2. Stir in pecans and pour into greased 9 x 13-inch (23 x 33 cm) baking pan.
3. Bake at 350° (176° C) for 35 minutes. Cool and cut into squares.

So easy and so very good!

Rainbow Cookie Bars

½ cup (1 stick) butter	125 ml
2 cups graham cracker crumbs	500 ml
1 (14 ounce) can sweetened condensed milk	1 (420 g)
⅔ cup flaked coconut	160 ml
1 cup chopped pecans	250 ml
1 cup M & M candies	250 ml

1. In 9 x 13-inch (23 x 33 cm) baking pan, melt butter in oven. Sprinkle crumbs over butter and pour condensed milk over crumbs.
2. Top with remaining ingredients and press down firmly.
3. Bake at 350° (176° C) for 25 to 30 minutes or until light brown. Cool and cut into bars.

When making these one time, I realized I was missing MMs so I substituted white chocolate bits and they were great (just not "rainbow").

Pecan Cream Cheese Squares

1 (18 ounce) package yellow cake mix	1 (520 g)
3 eggs, divided	3
½ cup (1 stick) butter, softened	125 ml
2 cups chopped pecans	500 ml
1 (8 ounce) package cream cheese, softened	1 (228 g)
3⅔ cups powdered sugar	910 ml

1. In mixing bowl, combine cake mix, 1 egg and butter. Stir in pecans and mix well. Press into greased 9 x 13-inch (23 x 33 cm) baking pan.
2. In mixing bowl, beat cream cheese, sugar and remaining eggs until smooth. Pour over pecan mixture.
3. Bake at 350° (176° C) for 55 minutes or until golden brown. Cool and cut into squares.

Peanut Butter Brownies

1 (21 ounce) package brownie mix	1 (600 g)
1 cup peanut butter morsels	1 (250 g)

1. Prepare brownie mix according to package directions and stir in peanut butter morsels. Spoon mixture into greased 9 x 13-inch (23 x 33 cm) baking pan.
2. Bake at 350° (176° C) for 35 minutes. Cool and cut into squares.

Lemon-Angel Bars

1 (1 pound) package one-step angel food cake mix	1 (454 g)
1 (20 ounce) can lemon pie filling	1 (570 g)
⅓ cup butter, softened	80 ml
2 cups powdered sugar	500 ml
2 tablespoons lemon juice	30 ml

1. Combine cake mix and lemon pie filling and stir until well mixed. Pour into greased, floured 9 x 13-inch (23 x 33 cm) baking pan. Bake at 350° (176° C) for 25 minutes.
2. Just before cake is done, mix butter, powdered sugar and lemon juice and spread over hot cake.
3. When cool, cut into bars. Store in refrigerator.

Gooey Turtle Bars

½ cup (1 stick) butter, melted	125 ml
2 cups vanilla wafer crumbs	500 ml
1 (12 ounce) semi-sweet chocolate morsels	1 (340 g)
1 cup pecan pieces	250 ml
1 (12 ounce) jar caramel topping	1 (340 g)

1. Combine butter and wafer crumbs in 9 x 13-inch (23 x 33 cm) baking pan and press into bottom of pan. Sprinkle with chocolate morsels and pecans.
2. Remove lid from caramel topping and microwave on HIGH for 30 seconds or until hot. Drizzle over pecans.
3. Bake at 350° (176° C) for about 10 to 15 minutes or until morsels melt. Cool in pan. (Watch bars closely. You want chips to melt, but you don't want crumbs to burn.) Chill at least 30 minutes before cutting into squares.

Caramel-Chocolate Chip Bars

1 (18 ounce) package caramel cake mix	1 (520 g)
2 eggs	2
⅓ cup firmly packed light brown sugar	80 ml
¼ cup (½ stick) butter, softened	60 ml
1 cup semi-sweet chocolate chips	250 ml

1. Combine cake mix, eggs, ¼ cup (60 ml) water, brown sugar and butter in large bowl. Stir until thoroughly blended. Mixture will be thick.
2. Stir in chocolate chips. Spread in greased, floured 9 x 13-inch (23 x 33 cm) baking pan.
3. Bake at 350° (176° C) for about 25 to 30 minutes or until toothpick inserted in center comes out clean. Cool. (These bars are especially good when frosted with prepared caramel icing.)

Pumpkin Cupcakes

1 (18 ounce) package spice cake mix	1 (520 g)
1 (15 ounce) can pumpkin	1 (438 g)
3 eggs	3
⅓ cup oil	80 ml
⅓ cup water	80 ml

1. With mixer, blend cake mix, pumpkin, eggs, oil and water. Beat for 2 minutes.
2. Pour batter into 24 paper-lined muffin cups and fill three-fourths full.
3. Bake at 350° (176° C) for 18 to 20 minutes or until toothpick inserted in center comes out clean. (You might want to spread with commercial icing.)

Divine Strawberries

1 quart fresh strawberries	1 L
1 (20 ounce) can pineapple chunks, well drained	1 (570 g)
2 bananas, sliced	2
1 (18 ounce) carton strawberry glaze	1 (520 g)

1. Cut strawberries in half or in quarters if strawberries are very large.
2. Add pineapple chunks and bananas.
3. Fold in strawberry glaze and chill. This is wonderful served over pound cake or just served in sherbet glasses.

This makes such a bright, pretty bowl of fruit
– besides that, it's delicious.

Coffee Surprise

1 cup strong coffee	250 ml
1 (10 ounce) package large marshmallows	1 (284 g)
1 (8 ounce) package chopped dates	1 (228 g)
1¼ cups chopped pecans	310 ml
1 (8 ounce) carton whipping cream, whipped	1 (228 g)

1. Melt marshmallows in hot coffee. Add dates and pecans and chill.
2. When mixture thickens, fold in whipped cream.
3. Pour into sherbet glasses. Place plastic wrap over top and chill.

This is a super dessert – no slicing – no "dishing up"
– just bring it right from the frig to the table.

Kahlua Mousse

1 (12 ounce) carton whipped topping	1 (340 g)
2 teaspoons dry instant coffee (dry)	10 ml
5 teaspoons cocoa	25 ml
5 tablespoons sugar	75 ml
½ cup kahlua liqueur	125 ml

1. In large bowl, combine whipped topping, coffee, cocoa and sugar and blend well.
2. Fold in kahlua.
3. Spoon into sherbet dessert glasses. Place plastic wrap over dessert glasses until ready to serve.

Light, but rich and absolutely delicious.

Candy-Store Pudding

1 cup cold milk	250 ml
1 (3.4 ounce) package instant chocolate pudding mix	1 (100 g)
1 (8 ounce) carton whipped topping	1 (228 g)
1 cup miniature marshmallows	250 ml
½ cup chopped salted peanuts	125 ml

1. In a bowl, whisk milk and pudding mix for 2 minutes.
2. Fold in whipped topping, marshmallows and peanuts.
3. Spoon into individual dessert dishes. Place plastic wrap over top and chill.

A special family dessert!

Cherry Trifle

1 (12 ounce) pound cake	1 (340 g)
⅓ cup amaretto	80 ml
2 (20 ounce) cans cherry pie filling	2 (570 g)
4 cups vanilla pudding	1 L
1 (8 ounce) carton whipped topping	1 (228 g)

1. Cut cake into 1-inch (2.5 cm) slices. Line bottom of 3-quart (3 L) trifle bowl with cake and brush with amaretto.
2. Top with 1 cup (250 ml) pie filling, followed by 1 cup (250 ml) pudding. Repeat layers 3 times.
3. Top with whipped topping. Chill several hours.

Caramel-Amaretto Dessert

1 (9 ounce) bag small Heath bars, crumbled	1 (240 g)
30 caramels	30
⅓ cup amaretto liqueur	80 ml
½ cup sour cream	125 ml
1 cup whipping cream	250 ml

1. Reserve about ⅓ cup (80 ml) crumbled Heath bars. In buttered 7 x 11-inch (18 x 28 cm) dish , spread candy crumbs.
2. In a saucepan, melt caramels with amaretto. Cool to room temperature.
3. Stir in creams and whip until thick. Top with reserved candy crumbs, cover and freeze. Cut into squares to serve.

Strawberry-Angel Dessert

1 (6 ounce) package strawberry gelatin	1 (170 g)
2 (10 ounce) cartons frozen strawberries with juice	2 (284 g)
2 (8 ounce) carton whipping cream, whipped	2 (228 g)
1 large angel food cake	1

1. Dissolve gelatin in 1 cup (250 ml) boiling water and mix well. Stir in strawberries.
2. Cool in refrigerator until mixture begins to thicken. Fold in whipped cream. Break cake into pieces and place in 9 x 13-inch (23 x 33 cm) dish.
3. Pour strawberry mixture over cake. Refrigerate overnight. Cut into squares to serve.

Pavlova

3 large egg whites	3
1 cup sugar	250 ml
1 teaspoon vanilla	5 ml
2 teaspoons white vinegar	10 ml
3 tablespoons cornstarch	45 ml

1. Beat egg whites until stiff, then add 3 tablespoons (45 ml) COLD water. Beat again and add sugar very gradually while still beating. Continue beating slowly, add vanilla, vinegar and cornstarch.
2. On parchment-covered cookie sheet, draw 9-inch (23 cm) circle and mound mixture within circle.
3. Bake at 300° (149° C) for 45 minutes. LEAVE in oven to cool. To serve, peel paper from bottom while sliding pavlova onto serving plate. Cover with whipped cream and top with assortment of fresh fruit such as kiwi, strawberries, blueberries, etc.

Oreo Sunday

½ cup (1 stick) butter	125 ml
1 (19 ounce) package Oreos, crushed	1 (545 g)
½ gallon vanilla ice cream, softened	2 L
2 jars fudge sauce	2
1 (12 ounce) carton whipped topping	1 (340 g)

1. Melt butter in 9 x 13-inch (23 x 33 cm) pan. Reserve about ½ cup (125 ml) crushed Oreos for top and mix remaining with butter to form crust in pan. (Press into pan.)
2. Spread softened ice cream over crust (work fast) and add fudge sauce on top.
3. Top with whipped topping and sprinkle with remaining crumbs. Freeze.

A kid's favorite!

Grasshopper Dessert

26 Oreo cookies, crushed	26
¼ cup (½ stick) butter, melted	60 ml
¼ cup creme de menthe liqueur	60 ml
2 (7 ounce) jars marshmallow creme	2 (198 g)
2 (8 ounce) cartons whipping cream	2 (228 g)

1. Combine cookie crumbs and butter and press into bottom of greased 9-inch (23 cm) spring form pan. Reserve about ⅓ cup (80 ml) crumbs for topping.
2. Gradually add creme de menthe to marshmallow creme. Whip cream until very thick and fold into marshmallow mixture. Pour over crumbs.
3. Sprinkle remaining crumbs on top and freeze.

Ice Cream Dessert

19 ice cream sandwiches	19
1 (12 ounce) carton whipped topping, thawed	1 (340 g)
1 (11¾ ounce) jar hot fudge ice cream topping	1 (335 g)
1 cup salted peanuts	250 ml

1. Cut 1 ice cream sandwich in half. Place 1 whole and 1 half sandwich along short side of ungreased 9 x 13-inch (23 x 33 cm) pan. Arrange 8 sandwiches in opposite direction in pan.
2. Spread with half whipped topping. Spoon fudge topping by teaspoonfuls onto whipped topping. Sprinkle with ½ cup (125 ml) peanuts. Repeat layers with remaining ice cream sandwiches, whipped topping and peanuts. (Pan will be full.)
3. Cover and freeze. To serve, take out of freezer 20 minutes before serving.

Twinkie Dessert

1 (10 count) box twinkies	10
4 bananas, sliced	4
1 (5.1 ounce) package vanilla instant pudding	1 (145 g)
1 (20 ounce) can crushed pineapple, drained	1 (570 g)
1 (8 ounce) carton whipped topping	1 (228 g)

1. Slice twinkies in half lengthwise and place in buttered 9 x 13-inch (23 x 33 cm) pan, cream side up. Make a layer of sliced bananas.
2. Prepare pudding according to directions (using 2 cups (500 ml) milk), pour over bananas and add pineapple.
3. Top with whipped topping and refrigerate. Cut into squares to serve.

Creamy Banana Pudding

1 (14 ounce) can sweetened condensed milk	1 (420 g)
1 (3¾ ounce) package instant vanilla	
pudding mix	1 (410 g)
1 (8 ounce) carton whipped topping	1 (228 g)
36 vanilla wafers	36
3 bananas	3

1. In large bowl, combine condensed milk and 1½ cups (375 ml) cold water. Add pudding mix and beat well. Chill 5 minutes. Fold in whipped topping.
2. Spoon 1 cup (250 ml) pudding mixture into 3-quart (3 L) glass serving bowl. Top with wafers, bananas and pudding. Repeat layering twice, ending with pudding.
3. Cover and refrigerate.

This is a quick and easy way to make the old favorite banana pudding.

White Velvet

1 (8 ounce) carton whipping cream	1 (228 g)
1½ teaspoons unflavored gelatin	7 ml
⅓ cup sugar	80 ml
1 (8 ounce) carton sour cream	1 (228 g)
¾ teaspoon rum flavoring	180 ml

1. Heat cream over moderate heat. Soak gelatin in ¼ cup (60 ml) cold water.
2. When cream is hot, stir in sugar and gelatin until they dissolve and remove from heat.
3. Fold in sour cream and flavoring. Pour into individual molds, cover with plastic wrap and chill. Unmold to serve. Serve with fresh fruit.

Orange-Cream Dessert

2 cups crushed cream-filled chocolate cookies (about 20)	500 ml
⅓ cup butter, melted	80 ml
1 (6 ounce) package orange gelatin	1 (170 g)
1½ cups boiling water	375 ml
½ gallon vanilla ice cream, softened	2 L

1. In a bowl, combine cookie crumbs and butter and set aside ¼ cup (60 ml) crumb mixture for topping. Press remaining crumb mixture into greased 9 x 13-inch (23 x 33 cm) dish.
2. In large bowl, dissolve gelatin in water, cover and refrigerate for 30 minutes.
3. Stir in ice cream until smooth. Work fast. Pour over crust. Sprinkle with reserved crumb mixture and freeze. Remove from freezer 10 or 15 minutes before serving.

Fruit Fajitas

1 (20 ounce) can cherry pie filling	1 (570 g)
8 large flour tortillas	8
1½ cups sugar	375 ml
¾ cup (1½ sticks) butter	180 ml
1 teaspoon almond flavoring	5 ml

1. Divide fruit equally on tortillas, roll up and place in 9 x 13-inch (23 x 33 cm) baking dish.
2. Mix 2 cups (500 ml) water, sugar and butter in saucepan and bring to boil. Add almond flavoring and pour over flour tortillas.
3. Place in refrigerator and soak 1 to 24 hours. Bake 350° (176° C) for 20 minutes or until brown and bubbly. Serve hot or room temperature.

Mango Cream

2 soft mangos	**2**
½ gallon vanilla ice cream, softened	**2 L**
1 (6 ounce) can frozen lemonade, thawed	**1 (170 g)**
1 (8 ounce) carton whipped topping	**1 (228 g)**

1. Peel mangos and cut slices around seed and cut into small chunks.
2. In large bowl, mix ice cream, lemonade and whipped topping. Fold in mango chunks.
3. Quickly spoon mixture into parfait glasses or sherbets and cover with plastic wrap. Place in freezer.

Blueberry-Angel Dessert

1 (8 ounce) package cream cheese, softened	1 (228 g)
1 cup powdered sugar	250 ml
1 (8 ounce) carton whipped topping, thawed	1 (228 g)
1 (14 ounce) prepared angel food cake	1 (115 g)
2 (20 ounce) cans blueberry pie filling	2 (570 g)

1. In large mixing bowl, beat cream cheese and sugar and fold in whipped topping.
2. Tear cake into small 1 or 2-inch (2.5 cm) cubes. Fold into cream cheese mixture, spread evenly in 9 x 13-inch (23 x 33 cm) dish and top with pie filling.
3. Cover and refrigerate for at least 3 hours before cutting into squares to serve.

Brandied Fruit

2 (20 ounce) cans crushed pineapple	2 (570 g)
1 (16 ounce) can sliced peaches	1 (454 g)
2 (11 ounce) cans mandarin oranges	2 (312 g)
1 (10 ounce) jar maraschino cherries	1 (284 g)
1 cup brandy	250 ml

1. Let all fruit drain for 12 hours. For every cup of drained fruit, add ½ cup sugar. Let stand 12 hours.   Add brandy, spoon into large jar and store in refrigerator.
2. This mixture needs to stand in refrigerator for 3 weeks. Serve over ice cream.

Brandied Apples

1 loaf pound cake	1
1 (20 ounce) can apple pie filling	1 (570 g)
½ teaspoon allspice	2 ml
2 tablespoons brandy	30 ml
Vanilla ice cream	

1. Slice pound cake and place on dessert plates. In saucepan, combine pie filling, allspice and brandy. Heat and stir just until heated thoroughly.
2. Place several spoonsful over cake. Top with scoop of vanilla ice cream.

Baked Custard

3 cups milk	750 ml
3 eggs	3
¾ cup sugar	180 ml
¼ teaspoon salt	60 ml
1 teaspoon vanilla	2 ml

1. Scald milk. Beat eggs and add sugar, salt and vanilla.
2. Pour scalded milk slowly into egg mixture.
3. Pour into 2-quart (2 L) baking dish and sprinkle a little cinnamon on top. Bake at 350° (176° C) in hot water bath for 45 minutes.

Individual Meringues

1(1 pound) box powdered sugar	1 (454 g)
6 egg whites, room temperature	6
1 teaspoon cream of tartar	5 ml
½ teaspoon vanilla	2 ml
1 teaspoon vinegar	5 ml

1. With mixer, beat sugar and egg whites at high speed for 10 minutes. Add cream of tartar, vanilla and vinegar and beat another 10 minutes.
2. Spoon individual meringues on greased cookie sheet. Bake at 250° (121° C) for 15 minutes. Raise temperature to 300° (149° C) and bake another 12 minutes. Remove immediately from cookie sheet and store between sheets of wax paper in tightly closed containers.

Cinnamon Cream

1 (16 ounce) box cinnamon graham crackers	1 (454 g)
2 (5 ounce) packages instant French vanilla pudding mix	2 (142 g)
3 cups milk	750 ml
1 (8 ounce) carton whipped topping	1 (228 g)
1 (18 ounce) prepared caramel frosting	1 (520 g)

1. This dessert must be made day before serving. Line bottom of 9 x 13-inch (23 x 33 cm) casserole dish with graham crackers with one-third of graham crackers.
2. With mixer combine vanilla pudding and milk and whip until thick and creamy. Fold in whipped topping. Pour half pudding mixture over graham crackers. Top with another layer of graham crackers and add remaining pudding mixture.
3. Top with final layer of graham crackers. (You will have a few crackers left.) Spread frosting over last layer of graham crackers. Refrigerate overnight.

Lime-Angel Dessert

1 (6 ounce) package lime gelatin	1 (170 g)
1 (20 ounce) can crushed pineapple with juice	1 (570 g)
1 tablespoon lime juice, 1 tablespoon sugar	15 ml
1 (8 ounce) carton whipping cream, whipped	1 (228 g)
1 large angel food cake	1

1. Dissolve gelatin in 1 cup (250 ml) boiling water and mix well. Stir in pineapple and lime juice and sugar.
2. Cool in refrigerator until mixture thickens. Fold in whipped cream. Break cake into pieces and place in 9 x 13-inch (23 x 33 cm) dish.
3. Pour pineapple mixture over cake and refrigerate overnight. Cut into squares to serve.

Crazy Cocoa Crisps

24 ounces white almond bark	**685 ml**
2¼ cups cocoa crispy rice cereal	**560 ml**
2 cups dry roasted peanuts	**350 ml**

1. Place almond bark in double boiler, heat and stir while bark melts.
2. Stir in cereal and peanuts.
3. Drop by teaspoonful on cookie sheet. Store in airtight container.

Peanut Krispies

¾ cup (1½ sticks) butter	**180 ml**
2 cups peanut butter	**500 ml**
1 (16 ounce) box powdered sugar	**1 (454 g)**
3½ cups crispy rice cereal	**875 ml**
¾ cup chopped peanuts	**180 ml**

1. Melt butter in large saucepan. Add peanut butter and mix well.
2. Add powdered sugar, crispy rice cereal and peanuts and mix.
3. Drop by teaspoonsful on wax paper.

Scotch Crunchies

½ cup crunchy peanut butter	125 ml
1 (6 ounce) package butterscotch bits	1 (170 g)
2½ cups frosted flakes	625 ml
½ cup peanuts	125 ml

1. Combine peanut butter and butterscotch bits in large saucepan and melt over low heat. Stir until butterscotch bits melt.
2. Stir in cereal and peanuts and drop by teaspoonfuls on wax paper.
3. Refrigerate until firm. Store in airtight container.

White Chocolate Salties

8 (2 ounce) squares almond bark	8 (57 g)
1 cup salted Spanish peanuts	250 ml
3 cups thin pretzel sticks, broken up	750 ml

1. Place almond bark in top of double boiler, heat and stir until almond bark melts. Remove from heat and cool 2 minutes.
2. Add peanuts and pretzels and stir until coated.
3. Drop by teaspoonfuls on wax paper. Chill 20 minutes or until firm.

Crispy Fudge Treats

6 cups crispy rice cereal	**1.5 L**
¾ cup powdered sugar	**180 ml**
1¾ cups semi-sweet chocolate chips	**430 ml**
½ cup light corn syrup	**125 ml**
⅓ cup butter	**80 ml**

1. Combine cereal and sugar in large bowl and set aside. Place chocolate chips, corn syrup and butter in 1-quart (1 L) microwave-safe dish. Microwave, uncovered on high for about 1 minute and stir until smooth. If you have vanilla on hand, stir in 2 teaspoons (10 ml) vanilla.
2. Pour over cereal mixture and mix well.
3. Spoon into greased 9 x 13-inch (23 x 33 cm) pan. Refrigerate for 30 minutes and cut into squares.

Tumbleweeds

1 (12 ounce) can salted peanuts	1 (340 g)
1 (7 ounce) can potato sticks, broken up	1 (198 g)
3 cups butterscotch chips	750 ml
3 tablespoons peanut butter	45 ml

1. Combine peanuts and potato sticks in bowl and set aside.
2. In microwave, heat butterscotch chips and peanut butter at 70% power for 1 to 2 minutes or until they melt. Stir every 30 seconds. Add to peanut mixture and stir to coat evenly.
3. Drop by rounded tablespoonfuls on wax paper-lined baking sheet. Refrigerate until set, about 10 minutes.

Caramel Crunch

½ cup firmly packed brown sugar	125 ml
½ cup light corn syrup	125 ml
4 tablespoons butter (no butter)	60 ml
6 cups chex cereal	1.5 L
2 cups peanuts	500 ml

1. In large saucepan, heat sugar, syrup and butter. Heat until sugar and butter melt, stirring constantly.
2. Add cereal and peanuts and stir until all ingredients are well coated.
3. Spread mixture on lightly greased cookie sheet and bake at 250° (121° C) for 30 minutes. Stir occasionally while baking. Cool and store in airtight container.

Butterscotch Peanuts

1 (12 ounce) package butterscotch morsels — 1 (340 g)
2 cups chow mein noodles — 500 ml
1 cup dry roasted peanuts — 250 ml

1. In saucepan, heat butterscotch morsels over low heat until they completely melt.
2. Add noodles and peanuts and stir until each piece is coated. Drop from teaspoonful on wax paper. Cool and store in airtight container.

Peanut Clusters

1 (24 ounce) package almond bark — 1 (685 g)
1 (12 ounce) package milk chocolate chips — 1 (340 g)
5 cups salted peanuts — 1.25 L

1. In double boiler, melt almond bark and chocolate chips.
2. Stir in peanuts and drop by teaspoonful on wax paper. Store in airtight container.

Roasted Mixed Nuts

1 pound mixed nuts — 454 g
¼ cup maple syrup — 60 ml
2 tablespoons brown sugar — 15 ml
1 (1 ounce) envelope ranch-style salad dressing mix — 1 (28 g)

1. In a bowl, combine nuts and maple syrup and mix well.
2. Sprinkle with brown sugar and salad dressing mix and stir gently to coat. Spread in greased 10 x 15-inch (25 x 38 cm) baking pan.
3. Bake at 300° (149° C) for 25 minutes or until light brown and cool.

Spiced Pecans

2 cups sugar	**500 ml**
2 teaspoons cinnamon	**10 ml**
1 teaspoon ground nutmeg	**5 ml**
½ teaspoon ground cloves	**2 ml**
4 cups pecan halves	**1 L**

1. Combine sugar, cinnamon, nutmeg, cloves and ½ cup (125 ml) water and ¼ teaspoon (1 ml) salt. Mix well and cover with wax paper. Microwave on high for 4 minutes and stir.
2. Microwave another 4 minutes. Add pecans and quickly mix well. Spread out on wax paper to cool.
3. Break apart and store in covered container.

You can't eat just one!

Toasted Pecans

12 cups pecan halves	**12**
½ cup (1 stick) butter	**125 ml**
Salt	

1. Place pecans in large baking pan. Toast pecans at 250° (121° C) for 30 minutes. Slice butter and spread in hot pan. Coat pecans completely with butter by stirring several times.
2. After pecans and butter mix well, sprinkle with salt and stir.
3. Toast pecans 1 hour until butter absorbs and pecans are crisp. Stir often.

Sugared Pecans

½ cup packed brown sugar	125 ml
¼ cup sugar	60 ml
½ cup sour cream	125 ml
⅛ teaspoon salt	.5 ml
3 cups pecan halves	750 ml

1. Combine sugars and sour cream and stir over medium heat until sugar dissolves. Boil to soft-ball stage. Add salt and remove from heat.
2. Add pecans and stir to coat. Pour on wax paper and separate pecans carefully. They will harden after several minutes.

Honeycomb Pecans

2 cups sugar	500 ml
2 tablespoons honey	30 ml
2 teaspoons vanilla	10 ml
1 teaspoon rum flavoring	5 ml
3 cups whole pecans	750 ml

1. Combine sugar, ½ cup (125 ml) water and honey in saucepan and stir to mix. Bring mixture to a boil (do not stir) and cook to soft-ball stage (240°) (116° C). Remove from heat, add flavorings and cool to lukewarm. Beat with mixer 2 to 3 minutes or until mixture turns creamy.
2. Add pecans and stir until coated. Drop by heaping teaspoonfuls on wax paper and cool.

Cinnamon Pecans

1 pound shelled pecan halves	454 g
1 egg white, slightly beaten with fork	1
2 tablespoons cinnamon	30 ml
¾ cup sugar	180 ml

1. Combine pecan halves with egg white and mix well. Sprinkle with mixture of cinnamon and sugar. Stir until all pecans are coated.
2. Spread on cookie sheet and bake at 325° (163° C) for about 20 minutes. Cool and store in covered container.

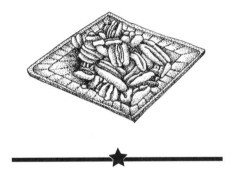

Fun-to-Make Sweet Pickles

1 quart whole sour pickles	1 L
3¼ cups sugar	810 ml
1 clove garlic, finely chopped	1
½ teaspoon ground cloves	2 ml

1. Pour off liquid from pickles and discard. Slice pickles in ¼-inch (.5 cm) slices and place in large bowl. Add sugar, garlic and cloves. Mix and leave at room temperature until sugar dissolves.
2. Spoon all back into jar. Seal and refrigerate. Ready to eat after 3 days.

Sweet and Sour Pickles

1 quart dill pickles, sliced, with juice	1 L
1½ cups sugar	375 ml
½ cup white vinegar	125 ml
¾ teaspoon mustard seeds	4 ml

1. Set aside juice. Place pickles in bowl and cover with sugar. Soak overnight.
2. Place pickles back in jar.
3. Heat juice, vinegar and mustard seeds to boiling point and pour over pickles. Let stand overnight.

Chocolate Crunchies

1 (20 ounce) squares chocolate-flavored candy coating	1 (570 g)
1 cup light corn syrup	250 ml
¼ cup (½ stick) butter	60 ml
2 teaspoons vanilla	10 ml
1 (7.2 ounce) package crispy rice cereal	1 (200 g)

1. Combine chocolate candy coating, corn syrup and butter in top of double boiler. Heat on low and cook until coating melts. Remove from heat and stir in vanilla.
2. Place cereal in large mixing bowl, pour chocolate mixture on top and stir until well coated.
3. Quickly spoon mixture into buttered 9 x 13-inch (23 x 33 cm) dish and press firmly with back of spoon. Cool completely and cut into bars.

Tiger Butter

1 pound white chocolate or almond bark	**454 g**
½ cup chunky peanut butter	**125 ml**
1 cup semi-sweet chocolate morsels	**250 ml**

1. Line 15 x 10-inch (38 x 25 cm) jelly-roll pan with wax paper. Heat white chocolate in microwave-safe bowl on high 1 to 2 minutes or until it melts. Stir until smooth.
2. Add peanut butter and microwave on high until it melts. Stir again until smooth. Spread mixture evenly into prepared pan.
3. In another microwave-safe bowl melt chocolate morsels on high. Pour chocolate over peanut butter mixture and swirl through with knife until you get desired effect. Refrigerate several hours until firm. Break into pieces.

Macadamia Candy

2 (3 ounce) jars macadamia nuts   2 (85 g)
1 (20 ounce) package white almond bark   1 (570 g)
¾ cup flaked coconut   180 ml

1. Heat dry skillet, toast nuts until slightly golden and set aside. (Some brands of macadamia nuts are already toasted.) Set aside.
2. In double boiler, melt 12 squares almond bark. As soon as almond bark melts, pour in macadamia nuts and coconut in and stir well.
3. Place wax paper on cookie sheet, pour candy on wax paper and spread out. Refrigerate 30 minutes to set. Break unto pieces.

When I want to make a candy that is special and one that most people have not eaten, this is the candy I make. And is it ever great!

Chocolate Peanut Butter Drops

1 cup sugar   250 ml
½ cup light corn syrup   125 ml
¼ cup honey   60 ml
1 (12 ounce) jar chunky peanut butter   1 (340 g)
4 cups chocolate-flavored frosted
    corn puff cereal   1 L

1. Combine sugar, corn syrup and peanut butter in Dutch oven. Bring to boil and stir constantly.
2. Remove from heat and add peanut butter and stir until it blends.
3. Stir in cereal, drop by tablespoonfuls on wax paper and cool.

White Chocolate Fudge

1 (8 ounce) package cream cheese, softened	1 (228 g)
4 cups powdered sugar	1 L
1½ teaspoons vanilla extract	7 L
12 ounces almond bark, melted	340 g
¾ cup chopped pecans	180 ml

1. Beat cream cheese at medium speed with mixer until smooth. Gradually add sugar and vanilla and beat well.
2. Stir in melted almond bark and pecans. Spread into buttered 8-inch square pan. Refrigerate until firm. Cut into small squares.

This is a little different slant to fudge
– really creamy and really good!

Creamy Peanut Butter Fudge

3 cups sugar	750 ml
¾ cup (1½ sticks) butter	180 ml
⅔ cup evaporated milk	160 ml
1 (10 ounce) package	
peanut butter-flavored morsels	1 (284 g)
1 (7 ounce) jar marshmallow creme	1 (198 g)

1. Combine sugar, butter and morsels in large saucepan. Bring to boil over medium heat and stir constantly. Cover and cook 3 minutes without stirring. Uncover and boil 5 minutes (do not stir).
2. Remove from heat, add morsels and stir until morsels melt. Stir in marshmallow creme and 1 teaspoon vanilla.
3. Pour into buttered 9 x 13-inch (23 x 33 cm) pan. Place in freezer for 10 minutes.

Diamond Fudge

1 (6 ounce) package semi-sweet	
chocolate morsels	1 (170 g)
1 cup creamy peanut butter	250 ml
½ cup (1 stick) butter	125 ml
1 cup powdered sugar	250 ml

1. Cook morsels, peanut butter and butter in saucepan over low heat. Stir constantly just until mixture melts and is smooth. Remove from heat.
2. Add powdered sugar and stir until smooth.
3. Spoon into buttered 8-inch (20 cm) square pan and chill until firm. Let stand 10 minutes at room temperature before cutting into squares. Store in refrigerator.

Karo Caramels

2 cups sugar	500 ml
1¾ cups light corn syrup	430 ml
½ cup (1 stick) butter	125 ml
2 (8 ounce) cartons whipping cream	2 (228 g)
1¼ cups chopped pecans, toasted	310 ml

1. In saucepan, combine sugar, syrup, butter and 1 cup (250 ml) cream. Bring to a boil. While boiling, add second cup of cream. Cook to soft-ball stage.
2. Beat by hand for 3 to 4 minutes.
3. Add pecans and pour on buttered platter. Cut when cool.

Microwave Fudge

3 cups semisweet chocolate morsels	750 ml
1 (14 ounce) can sweetened condensed milk	1 (420 g)
¼ cup (½ stick) butter, sliced	60 ml
1 cup chopped walnuts	250 ml

1. Combine morsels, milk and butter in 2-quart (2 L) glass bowl. Microwave on MEDIUM 4 to 5 minutes and stir at 1½-minute intervals.
2. Stir in walnuts and pour into a buttered 8-inch (20 cm) square dish. Chill 2 hours and cut into squares.

Microwave Pralines

1½ cups packed brown sugar	375 ml
⅔ cup half-and-half cream	160 ml
Dash of salt	
2 tablespoons melted butter	30 ml
1⅔ cups pecans, chopped	410 ml

1. Combine brown sugar, cream and salt in deep glass dish and mix well. Blend in butter. Microwave on high for 10 minutes, stir once and add pecans
2. Cool for 1 minute. Beat by hand until creamy and thick about 4 to 5 minutes. The mixture will lose some of its gloss.
3. Drop by tablespoonful on wax paper.

Peanut Brittle

2 cups sugar	500 ml
½ cup light corn syrup	125 ml
2 cups dry-roasted peanuts	500 ml
1 tablespoon butter	15 ml
1 teaspoon baking soda	5 ml

1. Combine sugar and corn syrup in saucepan. Cook over low heat, stirring constantly until sugar dissolves. Cover and cook over medium heat another 2 minutes.
2. Uncover, add peanuts and cook stirring occasionally to hard-crack stage (300°) (149° C). Stir in butter and baking soda. Pour into buttered jelly-roll pan and spread thinly.
3. Cool and break into pieces.

Peanut Butter Fudge

12 ounces chunky peanut butter	**340 g**
12 ounces package milk chocolate chips	**340 g**
1 (14 ounce) can sweetened condensed milk	**1 (420 g)**
1 cup chopped pecans or peanuts	**250 ml**

1. Melt peanut butter and chocolate chips.
2. Add condensed milk and heat. Add pecans and mix well.
3. Pour into 9 x 9-inch (23 x 23 cm) buttered dish.

Sugar Plum Candy

1¼ pounds vanilla-flavored	
almond bark, chopped	**570 g**
1½ cups red and green tiny marshmallows	**375 ml**
1½ cups peanut butter cereal	**375 ml**
1½ cups crispy rice cereal	**375 ml**
1½ cups mixed nuts	**375 ml**

1. In double boiler on low heat, melt almond bark.
2. Place marshmallows, cereals and nuts in large bowl. Pour melted bark over mixture and stir to coat.
3. Drop mixture by teaspoonfuls on wax paper-lined cookie sheet. Let stand until set and store in airtight container.

Easy Holiday Mints

1 (16 ounce) package powdered sugar	1 (454 g)
3 tablespoons butter, softened	45 ml
3½ tablespoons evaporated milk	52 ml
¼ to ½ teaspoon peppermint or almond extract	1 to 2 ml
Few drops of desired food coloring	

1. Combine all ingredients in large mixing bowl and knead mixture in bowl until smooth.
2. Shape mints in rubber candy molds and place on baking sheets. Cover with paper towel and dry. Store in airtight container.

Nutty Haystacks

1 pound candy orange slices, cut up	454 g
2 cups flaked coconut	500 ml
2 cups chopped pecans	500 ml
1 (14 ounce) can sweetened condensed milk	1 (420 g)
2 cups powdered sugar	500 ml

1. Place orange slices, coconut, pecans and milk in baking dish and cook at 350° (176° C) for 12 minutes or until bubbly.
2. Add powdered sugar and mix well.
3. Drop by teaspoonful on wax paper.

INDEX

Index

Index

Index

Index

COOKBOOKS PUBLISHED BY COOKBOOK RESOURCES, LLC

The Ultimate Cooking with 4 Ingredients
Easy Cooking with 5 Ingredients
The Best of Cooking with 3 Ingredients
Gourmet Cooking with 5 Ingredients
Healthy Cooking with 4 Ingredients
Diabetic Cooking with 4 Ingredients
4-Ingredient Recipes for 30-Minute Meals
Essential 3-4-5 Ingredient Recipes
The Best 1001 Short, Easy Recipes
Easy Slow-Cooker Cookbook
Essential Slow-Cooker
Quick Fixes with Cake Mixes
Casseroles to the Rescue
I Ain't On No Diet Cookbook
Kitchen Keepsakes/More Kitchen Keepsakes
Old-Fashioned Cookies
Grandmother's Cookies
Mother's Recipes
Recipe Keepsakes
Cookie Dough Secrets
Gifts for the Cookie Jar
All New Gifts for the Cookie Jar
Gifts in a Pickle Jar
Muffins In A Jar
Brownies In A Jar
Cookie Jar Magic
Quilters' Cooking Companion
Miss Sadie's Southern Cooking
Classic Tex-Mex and Texas Cooking
Classic Southwest Cooking
The Great Canadian Cookbook
The Best of Lone Star Legacy Cookbook
Cookbook 25 Years
Pass the Plate
Texas Longhorn Cookbook
Trophy Hunters' Guide To Cooking
Mealtimes and Memories
Holiday Recipes
Homecoming
Little Taste of Texas
Little Taste of Texas II
Texas Peppers
Southwest Sizzler
Southwest Olé
Class Treats
Leaving Home
Easy Desserts
Bake Sale Best Sellers

cookbook
resources LLC
www.cookbookresources.com